Cooking Club of America

# Great Grilling & Casual Cookouts

Special Edition for the
Cooking Club of America®
Cooking Arts Collection™

# GREAT GRILLING & CASUAL COOKOUTS

COOKING ARTS COLLECTION™

Mike Vail
**Vice President, Marketing and Business Development**

Tom Carpenter
**Director of Book and New Media Development**

**Better Homes and Gardens® Books**
**An imprint of Meredith® Books**

Editors: Kristi Fuller, Lisa Holderness
Contributing Editors: Nancy Verde Barr, Jennifer Darling, Karen Levin, Joan Moravek, Carol Munson, Mary Williams, Spectrum Communication Services Inc.
Contributing Writer: Lisa Kingsley
Designer: Craig Hanken
Copy Chief: Catherine Hamrick
Copy and Production Editor: Terri Fredrickson
Contributing Copy Editors: Marcia Gilmer, Jennifer Speer Ramundt
Contributing Proofreaders: Gretchen Kauffman, Susan J. Kling, Sheila Mauck, Beth Popplewell, Margaret Smith
Electronic Production Coordinator: Paula Forest
Editorial and Design Assistants: Judy Bailey, Mary Lee Gavin, Karen Schirm
Test Kitchen Director: Sharon Stilwell
Test Kitchen Product Supervisor: Marilyn Cornelius
Food Stylists: Lynn Blanchard, Dianna Nolin, Janet Pittman
Photographers: Jim Krantz, Kritsada Panichgul
Prop Stylists: Nancy Wall Hopkins, Karen Johnson
Production Director: Douglas M. Johnston
Production Managers: Pam Kvitne, Marjorie J. Schenkelberg

**Meredith® Books**
Editor in Chief: James D. Blume
Design Director: Matt Strelecki
Managing Editor: Gregory H. Kayko
Director, Sales & Marketing, Retail: Michael A. Peterson
Director, Sales & Marketing, Special Markets: Rita McMullen
Director, Sales & Marketing, Home & Garden Center Channel: Ray Wolf
Director, Operations: George A. Susral

Vice President, General Manager: Jamie L. Martin

***Better Homes and Gardens®* Magazine**
Editor in Chief: Jean LemMon
Executive Food Editor: Nancy Byal

**Meredith Publishing Group**
President, Publishing Group: Christopher M. Little
Vice President, Consumer Marketing & Development: Hal Oringer

**Meredith Corporation**
Chairman and Chief Executive Officer: William T. Kerr

Chairman of the Executive Committee: E. T. Meredith III

Originally published as *Better Homes and Gardens® Fresh and Simple™ 5 o'clock Grill* and *Fresh and Simple™ Casual Cookouts*.


First Edition. Printing Number and Year: 5 4 3 2 1 04 03 02 01 00
ISBN: 0-696-21200-5

# contents

# ah! fresh-air dining

**During the week, a casual dinner with friends or a simple family meal doesn't have to turn into a major production. Grilling outdoors keeps preparation simple and cleanup minimal for the cook under time constraints. Better yet, it keeps the kitchen cool. The notable difference in *Great Grilling & Casual Cookouts* is the use of fresh, innovative flavors created from easy-to-find produce and seasonings. Besides, what better way to unwind after working all day than cooking outdoors in the fresh air and enjoying a great meal?**

# a passion for poultry

# chicken & prosciutto roll-ups

**This pretty dish takes the Italian technique braciola—thin slices of meat wrapped around savories such as Italian ham, cheese, artichokes, spinach, and herbs—and applies it to chicken. Serve the attractive spirals with fresh spinach fettuccine.**



**Prep: 25 minutes Grill: 15 minutes**
**Makes 4 servings**

- ¼ cup dry white wine
- 2 teaspoons snipped fresh thyme or ½ teaspoon dried thyme, crushed
- 4 medium skinless, boneless chicken breast halves (about 1 pound total)
- 4 thin slices prosciutto (about 1 ounce total), trimmed of fat
- 2 ounces fontina cheese, thinly sliced
- ½ of a 7-ounce jar roasted red sweet peppers, cut into thin strips (about ½ cup)
- Fresh thyme (optional)

For sauce, in a small bowl combine wine and the 2 teaspoons fresh or ½ teaspoon dried thyme. Set aside.

Rinse chicken; pat dry. Place a chicken piece between 2 pieces of plastic wrap. Using the flat side of a meat mallet, pound the chicken lightly into a rectangle about ⅛ inch thick. Remove plastic wrap. Repeat with remaining chicken pieces.

Place a slice of prosciutto and one-fourth of the cheese on each chicken piece. Arrange one-fourth of the roasted peppers on cheese near bottom edge of chicken. Starting from bottom edge, roll up jelly-roll style; secure with wooden toothpicks. (At this point, chicken may be individually wrapped in plastic wrap and refrigerated up to 4 hours.)

Grill chicken on the rack of an uncovered grill directly over medium heat for 15 to 17 minutes or until chicken is tender and no longer pink, turning to cook evenly and brushing twice with sauce. If desired, garnish with additional fresh thyme.

Nutrition facts per serving: 214 cal., 9 g total fat (4 g sat. fat), 76 mg chol., 294 mg sodium, 2 g carbo., 0 g fiber, 27 g pro. Daily values: 14% vit. A, 85% vit. C, 7% calcium, 7% iron

# chicken caribbean

**Experience the islands without venturing off your landlocked patio. Fresh basil (try cinnamon basil if you can find it) infuses its aroma and peppery-clove flavor into the slightly sweet coconut-orange sauce—perfect with the spicy jerk-seasoned chicken.**



- **4 medium skinless, boneless chicken breast halves (about 1 pound total)**
- **½ teaspoon Jamaican jerk seasoning**
- **½ cup canned coconut milk**
- **¼ cup orange juice**
- **2 tablespoons snipped fresh basil**
- **1 teaspoon finely shredded orange peel (optional)**
- **2 cups hot cooked rice**

**Start to finish: 25 minutes**
**Makes 4 servings**

Rinse chicken; pat dry. Rub both sides of chicken with jerk seasoning. Grill chicken on the rack of an uncovered grill directly over medium heat 12 to 15 minutes or until chicken is no longer pink, turning once.

Meanwhile, for sauce, in a small saucepan combine coconut milk, orange juice, and 1 tablespoon of the basil. Bring to boiling; reduce heat. Simmer, uncovered, about 5 minutes or until reduced to ½ cup.

If desired, stir the orange peel into cooked rice. Serve chicken and sauce over rice. Sprinkle with the remaining basil.

Nutrition facts per serving: 287 cal., 9 g total fat (6 g sat. fat), 59 mg chol., 85 mg sodium, 25 g carbo., 0 g fiber, 24 g pro. Daily values: 2% vit. A, 13% vit. C, 2% calcium, 13% iron

## seasoned the right way

Marinades and rubs boost the flavor of grilled meats. Marinade, a liquid seasoned with herbs and spices, also can tenderize meat if it contains an acidic ingredient, such as lemon juice, yogurt, wine, or vinegar, or an enzyme found in papaya, ginger, pineapple, and figs. A rub is simply a blend of fresh or dried herbs or spices that's rubbed onto uncooked meats. For more rubs, marinades, and sauces, see pages 87 to 91.

# chicken with roquefort sauce

**Roquefort—the king of French blues—is a sheep's milk cheese that, by law, must be aged at least two months in the limestone caves of Roquefort in the South of France. Serve this dish with some French bread, a crisp green salad, and a dry white wine.**



**Prep: 12 minutes Grill: 12 minutes**
**Makes 4 servings**

- ½ cup plain fat-free yogurt
- ¼ cup chopped red onion
- 2 tablespoons crumbled Roquefort or other blue cheese
- 1 tablespoon snipped fresh chives
- ⅛ teaspoon white pepper
- 2 ripe small pears, halved lengthwise, cored, and stemmed
- Lemon juice
- 4 medium skinless, boneless chicken breast halves (about 1 pound total)

For sauce, in a small bowl combine yogurt, onion, Roquefort, chives, and white pepper. Cover and refrigerate until ready to serve. Brush the cut sides of pears with lemon juice. Set aside.

Rinse chicken; pat dry. Sprinkle with salt and pepper. Grill chicken on the rack of an uncovered grill directly over medium heat for 5 minutes. Turn chicken. Add pears to grill, cut sides down. Grill chicken and pears for 7 to 10 minutes or until chicken is tender and no longer pink. Serve chicken and pears with sauce.

Nutrition facts per serving: 199 cal., 5 g total fat (2 g sat. fat), 63 mg chol., 168 mg sodium, 14 g carbo., 2 g fiber, 25 g pro. Daily values: 2% vit. A, 9% vit. C, 8% calcium, 6% iron

# raspberry chicken with plantains

**Plantains are a starchier, less-sweet cousin of the beloved banana. Unlike bananas, though, they must be cooked before eaten. Here they're sautéed in butter, a little brown sugar, and vinegar to make a delicious side to smoky-sweet raspberry chicken.**



- **1 cup fresh raspberries (½ pint) or one 10-ounce package frozen unsweetened raspberries**
- **2 tablespoons granulated sugar**
- **1 teaspoon margarine or butter**
- **2 ripe plantains or firm bananas, sliced**
- **2 tablespoons brown sugar**
- **2 tablespoons white wine vinegar**
- **2 green onions, thinly sliced**
- **1 small fresh jalapeño pepper, seeded and finely chopped**
- **4 medium skinless, boneless chicken breast halves (about 1 pound total)**
- **Ti leaves (optional)**

**Start to finish: 30 minutes**
**Makes 4 servings**

For sauce, in a small saucepan combine raspberries and granulated sugar. Heat over low heat about 3 minutes or until the berries are softened. Press berries through a fine-mesh sieve; discard seeds.

For plantains, in a large nonstick skillet heat margarine or butter over medium heat. Add the plantains, if using, and cook and stir about 2 minutes or until plantains are lightly browned and slightly softened. Stir in bananas (if using), brown sugar, and vinegar; heat through. Remove from heat; stir in green onions and jalapeño pepper.

Rinse chicken; pat dry. Sprinkle with salt and pepper. Grill chicken on the rack of an uncovered grill directly over medium heat for 12 to 15 minutes or until chicken is tender and no longer pink, turning once. If desired, place a chicken breast on a ti leaf; spoon sauce over chicken. Serve with plantains.

Nutrition facts per serving: 300 cal., 5 g total fat (1 g sat. fat), 59 mg chol., 103 mg sodium, 45 g carbo., 4 g fiber, 23 g pro. Daily values: 13% vit. A, 48% vit. C, 2% calcium, 11% iron

# northwest chicken salad

**Perfect for an alfresco dinner on one of the first warm evenings of spring, this refreshing chicken salad features some of the season's best produce—crisp and tender greens, fresh asparagus, and sweet, juicy strawberries.**



- **2 medium skinless, boneless chicken breast halves (about 8 ounces total)**
- **1 recipe Raspberry Vinaigrette**
- **8 to 10 asparagus spears**
- **4 cups packaged shredded mixed salad greens**
- **6 to 8 strawberries**
- **1 pear, cored and sliced**
- **2 tablespoons chopped sweet onion**
- **8 to 10 pecan halves, toasted (optional)**

**Prep: 15 minutes  Marinate: 10 minutes  Grill: 12 minutes**
**Makes 2 servings**

Rinse chicken; pat dry. Place chicken in a plastic bag set in a shallow dish. Prepare Raspberry Vinaigrette; reserve half for dressing. Pour remaining vinaigrette over chicken; close bag. Marinate at room temperature for 10 to 15 minutes, turning bag once.

Drain chicken; reserve marinade. Grill the chicken on the rack of an uncovered grill directly over medium heat for 12 to 15 minutes or until chicken is no longer pink, turning and brushing once with marinade halfway through cooking. Discard marinade. Meanwhile, in a covered skillet cook the asparagus in a small amount of boiling water for 6 to 8 minutes or until crisp-tender. Drain. To serve, divide greens between 2 plates. Slice chicken; arrange over greens. Top with asparagus, berries, pear, and onion. Serve with reserved vinaigrette and, if desired, pecans.

**Raspberry Vinaigrette:** In a screw-top jar combine ¼ cup pear nectar; 2 tablespoons salad oil; 2 tablespoons raspberry vinegar; 1 teaspoon Dijon-style mustard; 1 teaspoon toasted sesame oil; ½ to 1 teaspoon dried basil, crushed; and ⅛ teaspoon pepper. Cover and shake well.

Nutrition facts per serving: 379 cal., 20 g total fat (3 g sat. fat), 59 mg chol., 131 mg sodium, 28 g carbo., 6 g fiber, 25 g pro. Daily values: 9% vit. A, 85% vit. C, 5% calcium, 15% iron

# chicken & vegetable salad

**One of the best things about the grill is its inherent ease. Here, a colorful medley of vegetables is grilled in a foil-pack right alongside honey-mustard chicken. No pan to clean up, no mess, no fuss—and delicious grilled flavor to boot!**



**Prep: 20 minutes Grill: 17 minutes**
**Makes 4 servings**

- 1 cup sliced cauliflower or broccoli flowerets
- 1 cup baby carrots
- 1 medium red and/or yellow sweet pepper, cut into strips
- 1 small red onion, thinly sliced and separated into rings
- ½ cup bottled honey-mustard salad dressing
- 4 medium skinless, boneless chicken breast halves (about 1 pound total)
- 6 cups packaged torn mixed salad greens
- 1½ cups cherry tomatoes, halved
- Honey-mustard dressing (optional)

Fold a 48×18-inch piece of heavy foil in half to make a 24×18-inch rectangle. Place cauliflower, carrots, sweet pepper, and onion in center of foil. Pour ¼ cup of the dressing over vegetables; toss to coat. Bring up 2 opposite edges of foil; seal with a double fold. Fold remaining ends to completely enclose vegetables, leaving space for steam to build.

Grill vegetables on the rack of an uncovered grill directly over medium heat for 5 minutes. Meanwhile, rinse chicken; pat dry. Brush chicken with remaining dressing. Place chicken on grill rack next to vegetables. Grill for 12 to 15 minutes or until chicken is tender and no longer pink and vegetables are tender, turning chicken and vegetables once.

To serve, divide the greens and tomatoes among 4 plates. Diagonally cut chicken into slices; arrange on top of greens. Divide vegetables among plates. If desired, drizzle salads with additional dressing.

Nutrition facts per serving: 320 cal., 19 g total fat (3 g sat. fat), 64 mg chol., 342 mg sodium, 15 g carbo., 4 g fiber, 24 g pro. Daily values: 102% vit. A, 109% vit. C, 5% calcium, 14% iron

# spicy chicken & star fruit

**It's a match made in heaven. The celestial star fruit (also called carambola) is a fitting addition to this chicken dish that's a little bit Italian (balsamic vinegar, olive oil, and rosemary) and a little bit Indian (cumin, coriander, and hot red pepper).**



**Prep: 15 minutes Grill: 12 minutes**
**Makes 4 servings**

- 2 tablespoons balsamic vinegar or red wine vinegar
- 1 tablespoon olive oil
- ½ teaspoon dried rosemary, crushed
- ¼ teaspoon ground cumin
- ⅛ teaspoon ground coriander
- ⅛ teaspoon black pepper
- Dash ground red pepper
- 2 star fruit (carambola), sliced
- 8 green onions, cut into 2-inch pieces, and/or 4 small purple boiling onions, cut into wedges
- 4 medium skinless, boneless chicken breast halves (about 1 pound total)
- 2 cups hot cooked rice
- 2 tablespoons peach or apricot preserves, melted (optional)

In a small bowl combine vinegar, olive oil, rosemary, cumin, coriander, black pepper, and red pepper. On eight 6-inch skewers alternately thread carambola and onions. Set aside.

Rinse chicken; pat dry. Grill the chicken on the rack of an uncovered grill directly over medium heat for 12 to 15 minutes or until chicken is tender and no longer pink, turning and brushing once with the vinegar mixture. Place kabobs on grill rack next to chicken the last 5 minutes of grilling, turning and brushing once with vinegar mixture.

Serve chicken and kabobs over rice. If desired, drizzle with preserves.

Nutrition facts per serving: 286 cal., 7 g total fat (1 g sat. fat), 59 mg chol., 57 mg sodium, 30 g carbo., 1 g fiber, 24 g pro. Daily values: 8% vit. A, 32% vit. C, 2% calcium, 17% iron

# chicken with mango chutney

**There are a variety of chutneys available on the market, but homemade is best—and who would have guessed something that seems so exotic could be so easy to make? This chutney features mangoes and is ready in less than 10 minutes.**



- **1 ripe mango, seeded, peeled, and sliced**
- **¼ cup dried currants or raisins**
- **¼ cup thinly sliced green onions**
- **2 to 3 tablespoons cider vinegar**
- **2 tablespoons brown sugar**
- **½ teaspoon mustard seed, crushed**
- **⅛ teaspoon salt**
- **1 pound skinless, boneless chicken thighs**
- **1 teaspoon five-spice powder**

**Start to finish: 25 minutes**
**Makes 4 servings**

In a medium saucepan combine half of the mango slices, the currants, green onions, vinegar, brown sugar, mustard seed, and salt. Bring to boiling; reduce heat. Simmer, covered, for 5 minutes. Remove from heat.

Meanwhile, chop the remaining mango slices; set aside. Rinse chicken; pat dry. Rub both sides of chicken with five-spice powder. Grill chicken on the rack of an uncovered grill directly over medium heat for 10 to 12 minutes or until chicken is tender and no longer pink, turning once.

To serve, stir the chopped mango into the cooked mango mixture. Serve with chicken.

Nutrition facts per serving: 205 cal., 6 g total fat (2 g sat. fat), 54 mg chol., 125 mg sodium, 22 g carbo., 2 g fiber, 17 g pro. Daily values: 22% vit. A, 26% vit. C, 3% calcium, 10% iron

# middle-eastern grilled chicken

**The cucumber sauce served alongside this grilled chicken has nuances of tsatsiki, the yogurt, cucumber, and garlic sauce served at taverns on the Greek isles. Cucumbers are added to half of the spiced yogurt; the remaining half doubles as a brush-on.**



**Prep: 12 minutes Grill: 15 minutes**
**Makes 4 servings**

- 1 8-ounce carton plain fat-free yogurt
- 1 small onion, finely chopped
- 1 tablespoon snipped fresh oregano or savory or 1 teaspoon dried oregano or savory, crushed
- 1½ teaspoons bottled minced garlic
- 1 teaspoon sesame seed, toasted
- ½ teaspoon ground cumin
- ¼ teaspoon ground turmeric (optional)
- ⅛ teaspoon salt
- 1 small cucumber, seeded and chopped (about ⅔ cup)
- 4 medium skinless, boneless chicken breast halves (about 1 pound total)
- Hot cooked couscous (optional)

In a medium bowl combine yogurt, onion, oregano, garlic, sesame seed, cumin, turmeric (if desired), and salt. Transfer half of the yogurt mixture to a small bowl and stir in cucumber; cover and refrigerate until ready to serve. Set the remaining yogurt mixture aside.

Rinse chicken; pat dry. In a grill with a cover arrange preheated coals around a drip pan.* Test for medium heat above pan. Place chicken on grill rack over pan. Spoon the remaining yogurt mixture over chicken. Cover and grill for 15 to 18 minutes or until chicken is tender and no longer pink.

Serve chicken with the cucumber mixture and, if desired, couscous.

Nutrition facts per serving: 169 cal., 4 g total fat (1 g sat. fat), 60 mg chol., 166 mg sodium, 7 g carbo., 0 g fiber, 26 g pro. Daily values: 1% vit. A, 4% vit. C, 11% calcium, 9% iron

*Note: If using a gas grill, follow the manufacturer's directions for cooking by indirect heat (see tip box page 44 for explanation of indirect versus direct grilling).*

# pineapple-rum turkey kabobs

**Lemongrass—an essential ingredient in Indonesian and Thai cooking—imparts a woodsy, lemony flavor to the marinade for these kabobs. If you can't find fresh lemongrass at your grocery store, look for it at almost any Asian market.**



- **12 ounces turkey breast tenderloin steaks or boneless turkey breast**
- **⅓ cup unsweetened pineapple juice**
- **3 tablespoons rum or unsweetened pineapple juice**
- **1 tablespoon brown sugar**
- **1 tablespoon finely chopped lemongrass or 2 teaspoons finely shredded lemon peel**
- **1 tablespoon olive oil**
- **1 medium red onion, cut into thin wedges**
- **2 nectarines or 3 plums, pitted and cut into thick slices**
- **1½ cups fresh or canned pineapple chunks**
- **Hot cooked rice (optional)**

**Prep: 15 minutes Marinate: 4 hours Grill: 12 minutes
Makes 4 servings**

Rinse turkey; pat dry. Cut into 1-inch cubes. Place turkey in a plastic bag set in a shallow dish. For marinade, combine the ⅓ cup pineapple juice, the rum, brown sugar, lemongrass, and oil. Pour over turkey; close bag. Marinate in refrigerator for 4 to 24 hours, turning bag occasionally.

Drain turkey, reserving marinade. In a small saucepan bring marinade to boiling. Remove from heat. On four 12-inch skewers alternately thread turkey and onion. Grill kabobs on the rack of an uncovered grill directly over medium heat for 12 to 14 minutes or until turkey is tender and no longer pink, turning once and brushing occasionally with marinade.

Meanwhile, on four 12-inch skewers alternately thread nectarines or plums and pineapple. Place on grill rack next to turkey kabobs the last 5 minutes of grilling, turning and brushing once with marinade. If desired, serve turkey and fruit kabobs with rice.

Nutrition facts per serving: 229 cal., 6 g total fat (1 g sat. fat), 37 mg chol., 36 mg sodium, 23 g carbo., 2 g fiber, 17 g pro. Daily values: 5% vit. A, 26% vit. C, 2% calcium, 8% iron

# five-spice chicken kabobs

**The Middle East goes Far East. Five-spice powder—an aromatic combination of ground spices that includes star anise, ginger, cinnamon, cloves, and Szechwan peppers—lends the Arab-invented kabob a Chinese flavor.**



- **¼ cup frozen orange juice concentrate, thawed**
- **2 tablespoons honey**
- **1 tablespoon soy sauce**
- **¼ teaspoon five-spice powder**
- **Dash ground ginger**
- **1 pound skinless, boneless chicken breast halves or thighs**
- **1 cup fresh pineapple chunks or one 8-ounce can pineapple chunks (juice pack), drained**
- **1 medium green sweet pepper, cut into 1-inch pieces**
- **1 medium red sweet pepper, cut into 1-inch pieces**
- **2 cups hot cooked rice**

**Prep: 15 minutes Grill: 12 minutes**
**Makes 6 servings**

For glaze, in a small bowl combine orange juice concentrate, honey, soy sauce, five-spice powder, and ginger. Set aside.

Rinse chicken; pat dry. Cut into 1-inch pieces. On six 12-inch skewers alternately thread chicken, pineapple, green pepper, and red pepper.

Grill kabobs on the rack of an uncovered grill directly over medium heat for 12 to 14 minutes or until chicken is tender and no longer pink, turning once and brushing once with glaze. Brush with any remaining glaze. Serve with rice.

Nutrition facts per serving: 218 cal., 2 g total fat (1 g sat. fat), 40 mg chol., 210 mg sodium, 32 g carbo., 1 g fiber, 17 g pro. Daily values: 17% vit. A, 132% vit. C, 2% calcium, 10% iron

## perfect rice, every time

Rice, a pretty plain-flavored grain, is a natural accompaniment to grilled meats because it soaks up the savory juices of the meat. For 3 cups (four ¾-cup servings) cooked long-grain white rice, measure 2 cups of water into a medium saucepan; bring it to a full boil. If desired, add ¼ teaspoon salt to water. Slowly add 1 cup rice, stir, and return to boiling. Simmer, covered, for 15 minutes. Remove from heat; let stand, covered, for 5 minutes.

# szechwan chicken strips

**The longer you leave the chicken in its Szechwan-style (meaning spicy-hot!) marinade, the more intense flavor of chilies and garlic you'll get. Broccoli slaw mix and tomatoes make a refreshing and cooling accompaniment to the tongue-tingling chicken strips.**



**Prep: 15 minutes Marinate: 10 minutes Grill: 10 minutes**
**Makes 4 servings**

- **1 pound skinless, boneless chicken breast halves**
- **⅓ cup rice vinegar**
- **¼ cup hoisin sauce**
- **1 to 2 teaspoons Szechwan chili sauce or ½ teaspoon crushed red pepper**
- **½ teaspoon bottled minced garlic**
- **16 cherry tomatoes**
- **2 cups packaged shredded broccoli (broccoli slaw mix)**
- **1 tablespoon chopped peanuts**

Rinse chicken; pat dry. Cut into bite-size strips. Place the chicken in a plastic bag set in a shallow dish. For marinade, combine vinegar, hoisin sauce, Szechwan chili sauce, and garlic. Reserve half for dressing. Pour remaining marinade over chicken; close bag. Marinate in refrigerator at least 10 minutes or up to 2 hours, turning bag once.

Drain chicken, reserving marinade. On four 12-inch skewers thread chicken, accordion-style. Grill the kabobs on the rack of an uncovered grill directly over medium heat for 10 to 12 minutes or until chicken is tender and no longer pink, turning once and brushing twice with the marinade up to the last 5 minutes of grilling. Add the tomatoes to ends of skewers the last 2 to 3 minutes of grilling.

Serve kabobs over shredded broccoli. Drizzle with the dressing and sprinkle with peanuts.

Nutrition facts per serving: 205 cal., 4 g total fat (1 g sat. fat), 59 mg chol., 401 mg sodium, 16 g carbo., 2 g fiber, 23 g pro. Daily values: 8% vit. A, 51% vit. C, 2% calcium, 8% iron

# turkey-peach salad

**Fresh fruit and poultry are a pleasing pair with a natural lightness. Here, juicy grilled turkey breast, peaches, and plums are artfully served in a hollowed-out peach "bowl" and drizzled with a light-as-air lemon-poppy seed dressing made with yogurt.**



- **4 turkey breast tenderloin steaks (about 1 pound total)**
- **1 teaspoon olive oil**
- **2 peaches, pitted and cut up**
- **2 plums, pitted and sliced**
- **2 tablespoons lemon juice**
- **½ cup lemon low-fat yogurt**
- **2 tablespoons thinly sliced green onion**
- **¼ teaspoon poppy seed**
- **Mixed salad greens**

**Start to finish: 30 minutes**
**Makes 4 servings**

Rinse turkey; pat dry. Rub both sides of turkey with oil. Sprinkle with salt and pepper. Grill turkey on the rack of an uncovered grill directly over medium heat for 12 to 15 minutes or until turkey is tender and no longer pink, turning once. Cut turkey into bite-size strips.

Meanwhile, in a medium bowl combine the peaches and plums. Add lemon juice; toss gently to coat. For dressing, in a small bowl combine yogurt, green onion, and poppy seed. If necessary, stir in 1 to 2 teaspoons additional lemon juice to reach drizzling consistency.

Divide greens among 4 dinner plates. (For peach bowls, see note below.) Arrange turkey and fruit on top of greens. Drizzle with dressing.

Nutrition facts per serving: 209 cal., 4 g total fat (1 g sat. fat), 51 mg chol., 96 mg sodium, 20 g carbo., 2 g fiber, 24 g pro. Daily values: 6% vit. A, 22% vit. C, 5% calcium, 7% iron

*Note: To serve the salad in peach bowls, cut 2 large peaches in half crosswise; remove pits. Using a spoon, scoop out some of the pulp to create shallow "bowls." Place on top of salad greens and spoon turkey and fruit into peach halves. Drizzle with dressing.*

# border grilled turkey salad

**Try a fresh new twist on taco salad. Chili-and-lime-flavored strips of grilled turkey are served over crisp greens and drizzled with a hot pepper-spiced, dried-tomato vinaigrette. It's all topped off with crunchy crumbled tortilla chips.**



- **4 turkey breast tenderloin steaks (about 1 pound total)**
- **¼ cup lime juice**
- **1 teaspoon chili powder**
- **1 teaspoon bottled minced garlic**
- **¾ cup bottled dried tomato vinaigrette***
- **1 medium fresh jalapeño pepper, seeded and finely chopped**
- **4 cups packaged torn mixed salad greens**
- **1 cup peeled, seeded, and chopped cucumber or peeled and chopped jicama**
- **1 large tomato, coarsely chopped**
- **8 baked tortilla chips, broken into bite-size pieces**

**Prep: 15 minutes Marinate: 30 minutes Grill: 12 minutes**
**Makes 4 servings**

Rinse turkey; pat dry. Place turkey in a plastic bag set in a shallow dish. For marinade, combine lime juice, chili powder, and garlic. Pour over turkey; close bag. Marinate in refrigerator at least 30 minutes or up to 3 hours, turning bag occasionally.

Drain turkey, reserving marinade. Grill the turkey on the rack of an uncovered grill directly over medium heat for 12 to 15 minutes or until turkey is tender and no longer pink, turning once and brushing occasionally with marinade up to the last 5 minutes of grilling. Discard remaining marinade. Cut turkey into bite-size strips.

Meanwhile, for dressing, in a small bowl stir together tomato vinaigrette and jalapeño pepper. Combine greens, cucumber, and tomato; toss to mix. Divide greens mixture among 4 dinner plates; arrange turkey on top of greens. Drizzle with dressing and sprinkle with tortilla chips.

Nutrition facts per serving: 363 cal., 19 g total fat (3 g sat. fat), 79 mg chol., 402 mg sodium, 13 g carbo., 2 g fiber, 36 g pro. Daily values: 7% vit. A, 46% vit. C, 3% calcium, 14% iron

**Note: If you can't find dried tomato vinaigrette, substitute ⅔ cup bottled red wine vinaigrette and 2 tablespoons snipped, drained oil-packed dried tomatoes.*

# turkey steaks & vegetables

**Vegetable juice—with a few added ingredients—doubles as a basting sauce for turkey steaks. Serve these savory grilled turkey steaks and grilled vegetables with chewy Italian bread and a glass of Chianti.**



**Prep: 6 minutes Grill: 12 minutes**
**Makes 4 servings**

- ¼ cup vegetable juice
- 3 tablespoons mayonnaise or salad dressing
- 1 tablespoon snipped fresh chives or green onion tops
- 2 teaspoons snipped fresh thyme or ½ teaspoon dried thyme, crushed
- ½ teaspoon bottled minced garlic
- 4 turkey breast tenderloin steaks (about 1 pound total)
- 2 small zucchini, halved lengthwise
- 2 large roma tomatoes, halved lengthwise

For sauce, in a small bowl gradually stir vegetable juice into mayonnaise; stir in chives, thyme, and garlic. Set aside.

Rinse turkey; pat dry. Sprinkle with salt and pepper. Grill the turkey and halved zucchini and tomatoes, cut sides down, on the rack of an uncovered grill directly over medium heat for 6 minutes.

Turn turkey and vegetables; brush with sauce. Continue grilling for 6 to 9 minutes more or until turkey and zucchini are tender, turkey is no longer pink, and tomatoes are heated through,* brushing occasionally with sauce. Serve with any remaining sauce.

Nutrition facts per serving: 209 cal., 11 g total fat (2 g sat. fat), 56 mg chol., 200 mg sodium, 6 g carbo., 1 g fiber, 22 g pro. Daily values: 7% vit. A, 29% vit. C, 2% calcium, 11% iron

**Note: If the tomatoes are done before the turkey, remove the tomatoes from the grill and keep them warm.*

# barbecued turkey tenderloins

**Southern barbecue goes gourmet! These substantial sandwiches feature spicy grilled turkey tucked into crusty French rolls with grilled tomatillos and fresh spinach. Try accompanying them with sweet potato chips, a tasty alternative to regular chips.**



**Prep: 10 minutes Grill: 20 minutes**
**Makes 4 servings**

- ½ cup bottled onion-hickory barbecue sauce
- 1 small fresh jalapeño pepper, seeded and finely chopped
- 1 tablespoon tahini (sesame butter)*
- 4 tomatillos, husked and halved lengthwise, or ½ cup salsa verde
- 2 turkey breast tenderloins (about 1 pound total)
- 4 French-style rolls, split
- Spinach leaves

For sauce, in a small bowl combine barbecue sauce, jalapeño pepper, and tahini. Transfer half of the sauce to another bowl for basting. Reserve remaining sauce until ready to serve. On two 8- to 10-inch skewers thread tomatillos, if using. Set aside.

Rinse turkey; pat dry. Brush both sides of turkey with basting sauce. Grill turkey on the greased rack of an uncovered grill directly over medium heat about 20 minutes or until the turkey is tender and no longer pink, turning and brushing once with basting sauce. Place tomatillos on the grill rack next to the turkey the last 8 minutes of grilling or until tender, turning once. Thinly slice turkey and chop tomatillos.

Toast the rolls on the grill. To serve, fill the rolls with a few spinach leaves, the grilled turkey, and tomatillos or salsa verde. Spoon on the reserved sauce.

Nutrition facts per serving: 378 cal., 8 g total fat (2 g sat. fat), 50 mg chol., 776 mg sodium, 45 g carbo., 1 g fiber, 30 g pro. Daily values: 12% vit. A, 24% vit. C, 9% calcium, 25% iron

**Note: Tahini is a thick paste that is made by crushing sesame seeds. It it most often used in Middle Eastern dishes and can be found in the ethnic foods section of most supermarkets.*

# beef it up

# garlic steaks with nectarine-onion relish

**What's better than the smell of steak on the grill in the summertime? The aroma of garlic-studded beef on the grill. The mint-scented relish features one of summer's favorite fruits. Serve this steak with some crusty bread to soak up the delicious juices.**



**Prep: 25 minutes Grill: 8 minutes**
**Makes 4 servings**

- **4 boneless beef top loin steaks, cut 1 inch thick (about 1½ to 2 pounds total)**
- **6 cloves garlic, thinly sliced**
- **2 medium onions, coarsely chopped**
- **1 teaspoon olive oil**
- **2 tablespoons cider vinegar**
- **1 tablespoon honey**
- **1 medium nectarine, chopped**
- **2 teaspoons snipped fresh applemint, pineapplemint, or spearmint**
- **Fresh applemint, pineapplemint, or spearmint (optional)**

Trim fat from steaks. With the point of a paring knife, make small slits in steaks. Insert half of the garlic into slits. Wrap steaks in plastic wrap; let stand at room temperature up to 20 minutes. (For more intense flavor, refrigerate up to 8 hours.) Sprinkle with salt and pepper.

Meanwhile, for relish, in a large nonstick skillet cook onions and remaining garlic in hot oil over medium heat about 10 minutes or until onions are a deep golden color (but not brown), stirring occasionally. Stir in vinegar and honey. Stir in nectarine and the 2 teaspoons mint; heat through.

Grill steaks on the rack of an uncovered grill directly over medium heat to desired doneness, turning once. (Allow 8 to 12 minutes for medium-rare and 12 to 15 minutes for medium doneness.) Serve the relish with steaks. If desired, garnish with additional mint.

Nutrition facts per serving: 272 cal., 9 g total fat (3 g sat. fat), 97 mg chol., 108 mg sodium, 13 g carbo., 1 g fiber, 34 g pro. Daily values: 2% vit. A, 9% vit. C, 2% calcium, 27% iron

# rosemary beef with sweet pepper relish

**The head-clearing tang of horseradish and the mellow-but-hearty flavor of beef go well together. Here, they're even better joined with a rub of fresh rosemary, garlic, and olive oil. An onion-and-pepper relish conveniently cooks in a foil-pack along with the steaks.**



- **1 medium onion, thinly sliced**
- **1 red or yellow sweet pepper, cut into strips**
- **1 tablespoon red wine vinegar**
- **1 tablespoon olive oil**
- **⅛ teaspoon black pepper**
- **2 teaspoons snipped fresh rosemary**
- **2 teaspoons bottled minced garlic**
- **4 boneless beef top loin steaks, cut 1 inch thick (about 1 pound total)**
- **1 tablespoon prepared horseradish**

**Prep: 15 minutes Grill: 8 minutes**
**Makes 4 servings**

For relish, fold a 24×18-inch piece of heavy foil in half to make a 12×18-inch rectangle. Place onion and sweet pepper in center of foil. Drizzle vinegar and 2 teaspoons of the oil over vegetables; sprinkle with black pepper. Bring up 2 opposite edges of foil; seal with a double fold. Fold remaining ends to completely enclose vegetables, leaving space for steam to build. Set aside.

In a small bowl combine the remaining oil, the rosemary, and garlic. Trim fat from steaks. Rub steaks with rosemary mixture. Spread one side of the steaks with horseradish.

Grill steaks and relish on the rack of an uncovered grill directly over medium heat until steaks are cooked to desired doneness, turning steaks and relish once. (Allow 8 to 12 minutes for medium-rare and 12 to 15 minutes for medium doneness.) Spoon the relish over steaks.

Nutrition facts per serving: 198 cal., 9 g total fat (2 g sat. fat), 65 mg chol., 92 mg sodium, 7 g carbo., 1 g fiber, 23 g pro. Daily values: 13% vit. A, 58% vit. C, 2% calcium, 19% iron

# filet mignon with portobello sauce

**Just a splash of Madeira or port wine makes this buttery, meltingly tender steak-and-mushroom dish simply marvelous. Madeira and port are both slightly sweet Spanish wines flavored with a bit of brandy.**



**Prep: 15 minutes Grill: 8 minutes**
**Makes 4 servings**

- **4 beef tenderloin steaks, cut 1 inch thick (about 1¼ pounds total)**
- **1 teaspoon olive oil**
- **¼ teaspoon pepper**
- **2 large portobello mushrooms, halved and sliced**
- **8 green onions, cut into 1-inch pieces**
- **1 tablespoon margarine or butter**
- **⅓ cup beef broth**
- **2 tablespoons Madeira or port wine**

Trim fat from steaks. Rub both sides of steaks with oil and pepper. Grill steaks on the rack of an uncovered grill directly over medium heat to desired doneness, turning once. (Allow 8 to 12 minutes for medium-rare and 12 to 15 minutes for medium doneness.)

Meanwhile, for sauce, in a large skillet cook and stir mushrooms and onions in hot margarine over medium heat about 5 minutes or until vegetables are tender. Stir in broth and Madeira or port. Bring to boiling. Remove from heat. Thinly slice steaks diagonally and serve with sauce.

Nutrition facts per serving: 260 cal., 13 g total fat (4 g sat. fat), 80 mg chol., 160 mg sodium, 4 g carbo., 1 g fiber, 29 g pro. Daily values: 8% vit. A, 11% vit. C, 1% calcium, 31% iron

### ready, set, grill!

The cooking times in this book don't include time to heat up the coals in a standard grill—but you won't lose any time if you light the coals first so they can be heating while you're preparing the food. Traditional briquettes—once lit—take about 20 to 30 minutes to burn hot enough for cooking. They should be ash-gray in daylight or glowing red all over in darkness. Convenient self-lighting coals need just 5 to 10 minutes before they're ready to go. If you have a gas grill, check your owner's manual for times.

# beef & fruit salad

**For an exotic presentation, serve the fruit mixture in a kiwano (kee-WAH-noh) shell. Also called "horned melon," the kiwano has a jellylike pulp with a tart, yet sweet flavor likened to a combination of banana and cucumber.**



**Prep: 20 minutes Marinate: 30 minutes Grill: 8 minutes**
**Makes 4 servings**

- 12 ounces boneless beef sirloin steak, cut 1 inch thick
- ⅓ cup reduced-sodium teriyaki sauce or soy sauce
- ¼ cup lemon juice
- ¼ cup water
- 2 teaspoons toasted sesame oil
- ⅛ teaspoon bottled hot pepper sauce
- 3 cups shredded napa cabbage
- 1 cup torn or shredded sorrel or spinach
- 2 cups fresh fruit (choose from sliced plums, nectarines, or kiwi fruit; halved seedless grapes or strawberries; raspberries; and/or blueberries)
- 2 kiwanos (optional)

Trim fat from steak. Place steak in a plastic bag set in a shallow dish. For marinade, combine the teriyaki sauce, lemon juice, water, oil, and hot pepper sauce. Reserve ⅓ cup for dressing. Pour remaining marinade over steak; close bag. Marinate at room temperature up to 30 minutes, turning bag occasionally. (Or, marinate in refrigerator up to 8 hours.)

Drain steak, reserving marinade. Grill steak on the rack of an uncovered grill directly over medium heat to desired doneness, turning once and brushing occasionally with marinade up to the last 5 minutes of grilling. (Allow 8 to 12 minutes for medium-rare doneness and 12 to 15 minutes for medium doneness.) Discard any remaining marinade.

To serve, divide cabbage and sorrel among 4 dinner plates. Thinly slice steak diagonally. Arrange steak and fruit on top of greens. Drizzle with the dressing (and, if desired, pulp of kiwano fruit). If desired, serve fruit in kiwano shells.*

Nutrition facts per serving: 248 cal., 10 g total fat (3 g sat. fat), 57 mg chol., 307 mg sodium, 19 g carbo., 2 g fiber, 22 g pro. Daily values: 19% vit. A, 86% vit. C, 6% calcium, 19% iron

**Note: To serve in kiwano shells, cut each kiwano in half crosswise. Scoop out pulp.*

# beef & avocado tacos

**Try the real flavors of Mexico with these soft tacos filled with grilled sirloin, peppers, and onions. True caballeros enjoy their tacos and burritos made with carne asada, or "grilled meat," and a little picante sauce.**



- 2 tablespoons lemon juice
- 1 avocado, seeded, peeled, and cut into ½-inch cubes
- 1 pound boneless beef sirloin or eye round steak, cut 1 inch thick
- 1 medium onion, cut into wedges
- 2 fresh cubanelle, Anaheim, or poblano peppers, cut into 1-inch squares
- 1 tablespoon olive oil
- ½ cup picante sauce
- 2 cups shredded lettuce
- 4 7- to 8-inch flour tortillas

**Prep: 20 minutes Grill: 10 minutes**
**Makes 4 servings**

Drizzle lemon juice over avocado; toss gently to coat. Set aside.

Trim fat from steak. Cut steak into 2×1-inch thin strips. On four 12-inch skewers thread steak, accordion-style. On four 12-inch skewers alternately thread onion and peppers. Brush vegetables with oil.

Grill the kabobs on the rack of an uncovered grill directly over medium heat for 10 to 12 minutes or until steak is cooked to desired doneness, turning kabobs once and brushing occasionally with picante sauce.

To serve, divide the steak, onion, peppers, avocado, and lettuce among the tortillas. Fold tortillas over filling. If desired, serve with additional picante sauce.

Nutrition facts per serving: 425 cal., 24 g total fat (6 g sat. fat), 76 mg chol., 403 mg sodium, 24 g carbo., 3 g fiber, 30 g pro. Daily values: 7% vit. A, 105% vit. C, 5% calcium, 32% iron

# jalapeño beef kabobs

**Firecracker-hot but as sweet-as-pie, jalapeño pepper jelly adds tongue-tingling zing to these beef kabobs. Baby pattypan squash and tomatillos, with their green-tomato texture and lemon-apple essence, add even more interest.**



**Prep: 15 minutes Grill: 12 minutes**
**Makes 4 servings**

- **1 10-ounce jar jalapeño pepper jelly**
- **2 tablespoons lime juice**
- **½ teaspoon bottled minced garlic**
- **4 small purple or white boiling onions**
- **4 baby pattypan squash, halved crosswise**
- **1 pound boneless beef sirloin steak, cut 1 inch thick**
- **4 tomatillos, husked and cut into quarters**
- **½ medium red or green sweet pepper, cut into 1-inch squares**
- **Fresh snipped cilantro (optional)**
- **Hot cooked rice (optional)**

For glaze, in a small saucepan combine the jalapeño jelly, lime juice, and garlic. Cook and stir over medium heat until jelly is melted. Remove from heat.

In a small covered saucepan cook onions in a small amount of boiling water for 3 minutes. Add squash; cook for 1 minute more. Drain. Trim fat from steak. Cut steak into 1-inch cubes. On four 12-inch skewers alternately thread steak, onions, squash, tomatillos, and sweet pepper.

Grill the kabobs on the rack of an uncovered grill directly over medium heat for 12 to 14 minutes or until steak is cooked to desired doneness, turning kabobs once and brushing occasionally with glaze the last 5 minutes of grilling. If desired, stir cilantro into cooked rice and serve with kabobs. Serve with any remaining glaze.

Nutrition facts per serving: 444 cal., 11 g total fat (4 g sat. fat), 76 mg chol., 71 mg sodium, 61 g carbo., 2 g fiber, 27 g pro. Daily values: 9% vit. A, 54% vit. C, 4% calcium, 27% iron

# lemony flank steak

**Though it's rare to utter the words "light" and "beef" in the same breath, this refreshingly different dish is undeniably both. Lots of fresh lemon flavors the super-lean flank steak or top sirloin. Serve it with a side of grilled or steamed asparagus.**



- 1 1½-pound beef flank steak or boneless beef top sirloin steak
- 1 teaspoon finely shredded lemon peel
- ½ cup lemon juice
- 2 tablespoons sugar
- 2 tablespoons soy sauce
- 2 teaspoons snipped fresh oregano or ½ teaspoon dried oregano, crushed
- ⅛ teaspoon pepper
- Lemon slices (optional)
- Fresh oregano leaves (optional)

**Prep:** 15 minutes **Marinate:** 2 hours **Grill:** 12 minutes
**Makes** 3 servings

Trim fat from steak. Score steak on both sides by making shallow cuts at 1-inch intervals in a diamond pattern. Place steak in a plastic bag set in a shallow dish. For marinade, combine the lemon peel, lemon juice, sugar, soy sauce, oregano, and pepper. Pour over steak; close bag. Marinate in refrigerator at least 2 hours or overnight.

Drain steak, reserving marinade. Grill steak on the rack of an uncovered grill directly over medium heat to desired doneness, turning and brushing once with marinade halfway through cooking. (Allow 12 to 14 minutes for medium doneness.) Discard any remaining marinade.

To serve, thinly slice steak diagonally across the grain. If desired, garnish with lemon slices and fresh oregano leaves.

Nutrition facts per serving: 267 cal., 12 g total fat (5 g sat. fat), 80 mg chol., 357 mg sodium, 5 g carbo., 0 g fiber, 33 g pro. Daily values: 12% vit. C, 1% calcium, 21% iron

# peppercorn beef

**These savory steaks get much of their great flavor from the bite of fresh-cracked pepper. Using all black peppercorns works just fine, but a mix of black (the hottest), white (gentler), and pink (faintly sweet) peppercorns offers more variety of flavors.**



- **4 beef tenderloin steaks (about 1½ pounds total) or 1 to 1½ pounds boneless beef sirloin steak, cut 1¼ inches thick**
- **⅓ cup bottled oil and vinegar salad dressing**
- **⅓ cup dry red wine**
- **¼ cup snipped fresh garlic chives or ¼ cup snipped fresh chives plus 1 teaspoon bottled minced garlic**
- **1 teaspoon cracked multicolor or black peppercorns**

**Prep: 12 minutes Marinate: 15 minutes Grill: 14 minutes**
**Makes 4 servings**

Trim any fat from steak(s). Place meat in a plastic bag set in a shallow dish. For marinade, combine the salad dressing, wine, garlic chives, and pepper. Pour over steaks; close bag. Marinate meat at room temperature for 15 minutes, turning bag once. (Or, marinate steaks in refrigerator for 8 to 12 hours.)

Drain the steak(s), reserving marinade. Grill meat on the rack of an uncovered grill directly over medium heat to desired doneness, turning and brushing once with marinade halfway through cooking. (Allow 14 to 18 minutes for medium-rare and 18 to 22 minutes for medium doneness.) Discard any remaining marinade. If using sirloin steak, cut steak into 4 serving-size pieces.

Nutrition facts per serving: 287 cal., 16 g total fat (5 g sat. fat), 96 mg chol., 218 mg sodium, 1 g carbo., 0 g fiber, 32 g pro. Daily values: 2% vit. C, 28% iron

# southwest steak

**Marinating the meat overnight in an aromatic mélange of fresh ingredients makes this steak doubly good: It intensifies the delicious flavors, and the dish can be ready to eat in a flash on a weeknight. Serve it with cilantro-flecked rice or warmed flour tortillas.**



**Prep: 20 minutes Marinate: 6 hours Grill: 14 minutes**
**Makes 4 servings**

- **1 pound boneless beef sirloin steak, cut 1¼ to 1½ inches thick**
- **1 medium onion, chopped**
- **⅓ cup lime juice**
- **¼ cup snipped fresh cilantro**
- **3 fresh jalapeño peppers, seeded and finely chopped**
- **3 tablespoons water**
- **2 tablespoons cooking oil**
- **1 teaspoon ground cumin**
- **1 teaspoon bottled minced garlic**
- **½ teaspoon ground red pepper**
- **¼ teaspoon salt**
- **Snipped fresh cilantro (optional)**
- **Hot cooked rice (optional)**

Trim fat from steak. Place steak in a plastic bag set in a shallow dish. For marinade, combine onion, lime juice, 2 tablespoons of the cilantro, the jalapeño peppers, water, oil, cumin, garlic, red pepper, and salt. Pour over steak; close bag. Marinate in refrigerator for 6 hours or overnight, turning bag occasionally.

Drain steak, reserving marinade. Grill steak on the rack of an uncovered grill directly over medium heat to desired doneness, turning once and brushing occasionally with marinade up to the last 5 minutes. (Allow 14 to 18 minutes for medium-rare and 18 to 22 minutes for medium doneness.) Discard any remaining marinade. Sprinkle steak with the remaining 2 tablespoons cilantro. If desired, stir additional cilantro into cooked rice and serve with steak.

Nutrition facts per serving: 256 cal., 15 g total fat (5 g sat. fat), 76 mg chol., 148 mg sodium, 3 g carbo., 0 g fiber, 26 g pro. Daily values: 1% vit. A, 27% vit. C, 1% calcium, 22% iron

# spanish meat loaves

**Humble meat loaf goes haute cuisine, but retains its almost-universal appeal. These miniature loaves, flavored with pimiento-stuffed green olives and flat-leaf parsley and glazed with sweet-hot jalapeño pepper jelly, will charm their way into your repertoire.**



- **1 beaten egg**
- **¾ cup quick-cooking rolled oats**
- **½ cup pimiento-stuffed green olives, sliced**
- **¼ cup snipped Italian flat-leaf parsley or curly parsley**
- **¼ cup tomato paste**
- **¼ teaspoon pepper**
- **1 pound lean ground beef**
- **¼ cup jalapeño pepper jelly or apple jelly, melted**
- **1 medium tomato, chopped**
- **⅓ cup chunky salsa**
- **¼ cup chopped, seeded cucumber**
- **2 tablespoons sliced pimiento-stuffed green olives (optional)**
- **Lettuce leaves**
- **8 thin slices bread, toasted (optional)**

**Prep: 15 minutes Grill: 18 minutes**
**Makes 4 servings**

In a medium bowl combine the egg, rolled oats, the ½ cup olives, the parsley, tomato paste, and pepper. Add the ground beef; mix well. Form into four 4×2½×1-inch meat loaves.

Grill meat loaves on the rack of an uncovered grill directly over medium heat for 16 to 18 minutes or until meat is no longer pink, turning once. Brush with melted jelly; grill for 2 minutes more.

Meanwhile, for relish, in a small bowl combine the tomato, salsa, cucumber, and, if desired, the 2 tablespoons olives. Divide the lettuce and, if desired, bread slices among 4 dinner plates. Top with the meat loaves and relish.

Nutrition facts per serving: 362 cal., 16 g total fat (5 g sat. fat), 125 mg chol., 479 mg sodium, 31 g carbo., 2 g fiber, 26 g pro. Daily values: 15% vit. A, 47% vit. C, 4% calcium, 30% iron

# indian beef patties

**Try one of the many Indian breads with these meat patties. Look for chapati or roti (soft, unleavened, whole wheat bread); pappadam (paper-thin lentil crackers spiked with black peppercorns); or naan (soft, yeasted flatbread baked in a tandoor, or clay oven).**



- ½ cup plain low-fat yogurt
- ⅓ cup chopped, seeded cucumber
- ¼ cup finely chopped onion
- 1 medium fresh jalapeño pepper, seeded and chopped, or 2 tablespoons canned diced green chili peppers
- 1 tablespoon snipped fresh mint or 1 teaspoon dried mint, crushed
- ½ teaspoon ground cumin
- ½ teaspoon bottled minced garlic or ⅛ teaspoon garlic powder
- ¼ teaspoon salt
- 8 ounces lean ground beef, pork, or turkey

**Prep: 15 minutes Grill: 14 minutes**
**Makes 2 servings**

For sauce, in a small bowl stir together yogurt and cucumber. Cover and refrigerate until ready to serve.

In a medium bowl combine the onion, jalapeño pepper, mint, cumin, garlic, and salt. Add the ground beef; mix well. Form mixture into two ¾-inch-thick patties. Grill patties on the rack of an uncovered grill directly over medium heat for 14 to 18 minutes or until meat is no longer pink, turning once. Serve the sauce over patties.

Nutrition facts per serving: 238 cal., 12 g total fat (5 g sat. fat), 75 mg chol., 353 mg sodium, 8 g carbo., 1 g fiber, 24 g pro. Daily values: 2% vit. A, 27% vit. C, 11% calcium, 22% iron

## direct versus **indirect**

Direct grilling means food is placed on the rack directly over the coals. This method is preferred for fast-cooking foods (burgers, steaks, boneless chicken pieces, fish, and seafood). Indirect grilling means that a covered grill acts as an oven. A disposable drip pan is placed in the center of the charcoal grate and hot coals are arranged around it. This method is used for slower-cooking foods (roasts, whole or bone-in poultry, or ribs; or foods that may burn over direct heat, for example, rubs with fresh herbs or high-sugar sauces). Because of their speed, most of the recipes in this book call for direct grilling. See grilling charts on pages 178–181 for timings.

# beef & swiss sandwiches

**These sandwiches are a tantalizing fusion of juicy, horseradish-mustard-marinated steak on toasted rolls; tangy, melting Swiss cheese; and crunchy cabbage slaw flavored with caramelized sweet onions. Delicious!**



**Prep: 15 minutes Marinate: 6 hours Grill: 12 minutes**
**Makes 6 servings**

- 1 1- to 1¼-pound beef flank steak
- 1 medium sweet onion (such as Vidalia or Walla Walla), thinly sliced
- ½ cup bottled clear Italian salad dressing or oil and vinegar salad dressing
- 2 tablespoons horseradish mustard
- 6 French-style rolls, split
- 1½ cups packaged shredded cabbage with carrot (coleslaw mix) or shredded red cabbage
- 4 ounces thinly sliced Swiss cheese

Trim fat from steak. Score the steak by making shallow cuts at 1-inch intervals in a diamond pattern. Place steak and onion in a plastic bag set in a shallow dish. Combine dressing and mustard. Add to bag; close bag. Marinate in refrigerator for 6 to 24 hours, turning bag occasionally.

Drain steak and onion, reserving marinade. Fold a 24×18-inch piece of heavy foil in half to make a 12×18-inch rectangle. Place onion in the center of foil. Drizzle 2 tablespoons of the marinade over onion. Bring up 2 opposite edges of foil; seal with a double fold. Fold remaining ends to completely enclose onion, leaving space for steam to build.

Grill steak and onion on the rack of an uncovered grill directly over medium heat until steak is cooked to desired doneness, turning steak and onion and brushing steak once with marinade halfway through cooking. (Allow 12 to 14 minutes for medium doneness.) Discard any remaining marinade. Toast the rolls on the grill.

To serve, thinly slice steak diagonally across grain. Toss together onion and cabbage. Fill rolls with steak and onion mixture. Top with cheese.

Nutrition facts per serving: 394 cal., 22 g total fat (7 g sat. fat), 53 mg chol., 530 mg sodium, 25 g carbo., 1 g fiber, 24 g pro. Daily values: 18% vit. A, 16% vit. C, 19% calcium, 17% iron

# perfect pork & lamb

# southwest pork chops with corn salsa

**In late summer, when the corn is at its sweetest and the tomatoes are at their juiciest, these meaty pork chops crowned with a colorful, chunky salsa are unsurpassed for the freshest tastes of the season's best.**



**Prep: 20 minutes Grill: 8 minutes**
**Makes 4 servings**

- **¼ cup white wine vinegar**
- **3 tablespoons snipped fresh cilantro**
- **1 teaspoon olive oil**
- **1 cup fresh or frozen whole kernel corn**
- **3 plum-shaped tomatoes, chopped**
- **½ cup thinly sliced green onions**
- **1 small fresh jalapeño pepper, seeded and minced**
- **4 center-cut pork loin chops, cut ¾ inch thick**
- **Cactus leaves (optional)**

For sauce, combine 3 tablespoons of the vinegar, 1 tablespoon of the cilantro, and the olive oil. For salsa, thaw corn, if frozen. In a medium bowl combine corn, tomatoes, green onions, jalapeño pepper, the remaining vinegar, and the remaining cilantro. Set aside.

Trim fat from chops. Grill chops on rack of an uncovered grill directly over medium heat for 8 to 11 minutes or until chops are slightly pink in center and juices run clear, turning once and brushing occasionally with sauce. If desired, serve chops on cactus leaves. Serve with salsa.

Nutrition facts per serving: 201 cal., 9 g total fat (3 g sat. fat), 51 mg chol., 51 mg sodium, 14 g carbo., 2 g fiber, 18 g pro. Daily values: 7% vit. A, 35% vit. C, 8% iron

## particular about pork

Today's pork is leaner—and therefore lower in fat and calories—than ever before. Because there is so little fat, pork requires a little extra attention when being grilled to ensure tender, juicy meat. Closely check timings and temperatures in the recipes. Cook roasts and chops from the loin and rib sections to an internal temperature of 160° (medium-well) or 170° (well done). Cook ground pork and less-tender cuts such as sirloin or loin blade roasts and chops to 170° (well done) or until no pink remains.

# currant-glazed pork burgers

**Currant jelly and cloves—favorites for flavoring the Christmas ham—go casual for everyday eating in these savory pork burgers. Choose leafy greens such as Bibb, red-tip leaf, or romaine lettuce as a crisp accompaniment.**



- ¼ cup currant jelly
- 3 tablespoons catsup
- 1 tablespoon vinegar
- ⅛ teaspoon ground cinnamon
- Dash ground cloves
- 1 beaten egg
- 3 tablespoons fine dry bread crumbs
- 2 tablespoons chopped onion
- 2 tablespoons milk
- ¼ teaspoon salt
- ¼ teaspoon dried thyme, crushed
- ⅛ teaspoon pepper
- 1 pound lean ground pork
- 4 whole wheat hamburger buns, split
- 4 lettuce leaves

**Prep: 15 minutes Grill: 14 minutes**
**Makes 4 servings**

For sauce, in a small saucepan combine currant jelly, catsup, vinegar, cinnamon, and cloves. Cook and stir just until boiling. Remove from heat and keep warm.

In a medium bowl combine egg, bread crumbs, onion, milk, salt, thyme, and pepper. Add the ground pork; mix well. Form mixture into four ¾-inch-thick patties.

Grill patties on the rack of an uncovered grill directly over medium heat for 14 to 18 minutes or until meat is no longer pink, turning once. Toast the hamburger buns on the grill.

Place lettuce on bottoms of buns; top with patties. Spoon the sauce evenly over patties.

Nutrition facts per serving: 347 cal., 11 g total fat (4 g sat. fat), 107 mg chol., 612 mg sodium, 43 g carbo., 3 g fiber, 21 g pro. Daily values: 5% vit. A, 6% vit. C, 6% calcium, 18% iron

# smoky pork & mushroom kabobs

**These kabobs boast the flavors of fall: maple syrup, cider vinegar, hickory smoke, and sweet-tart apples. Choose a good cooking apple, such as Rome Beauty, York Imperial, Newtown Pippin, or Granny Smith.**



**Prep: 15 minutes Marinate: 10 minutes Grill: 14 minutes**
**Makes 4 servings**

- 1 pound lean boneless pork
- 8 ounces fresh mushroom caps
- 2 medium apples, cored and quartered
- 1 medium onion, cut into wedges
- ¼ cup maple-flavored syrup
- ¼ cup tomato paste
- 2 tablespoons cider vinegar
- ¼ to ½ teaspoon hickory smoke flavoring
- ⅛ teaspoon pepper

Trim fat from pork. Cut pork into 1½-inch cubes. Place the pork, mushrooms, apples, and onion in a plastic bag set in a shallow dish. For marinade, combine the syrup, tomato paste, vinegar, smoke flavoring, and pepper. Reserve ¼ cup marinade for dipping sauce. Pour remaining marinade over the pork, mushrooms, apples, onion; close bag. Marinate in refrigerator at least 10 minutes or up to 4 hours, turning the bag once.

Drain the pork mixture, reserving marinade. On four 12-inch skewers alternately thread pork, mushrooms, apples, and onion.

Grill kabobs on the greased rack of an uncovered grill directly over medium heat for 14 to 16 minutes or until the pork is slightly pink in the center and juices run clear, turning and brushing once with reserved marinade halfway through grilling. Serve with dipping sauce.

Nutrition facts per serving: 261 cal., 8 g total fat (3 g sat. fat), 51 mg chol., 54 mg sodium, 32 g carbo., 3 g fiber, 18 g pro. Daily values: 4% vit. A, 23% vit. C, 1% calcium, 16% iron

# canadian bacon pizza

**Pizza—on the grill? You bet! The intense, direct heat of the grill approximates that of a wood-fired pizza oven, imparting the pie's veggies and cheese with a pleasing smoke flavor, the Canadian bacon with real sizzle, and the crust with a delightful crunch.**



**Prep: 20 minutes Grill: 8 minutes**
**Makes 4 servings**

- 1 6-ounce jar marinated artichoke hearts
- 4 6-inch Italian bread shells (Boboli)
- ½ cup shredded fontina or mozzarella cheese (2 ounces)
- 4 slices Canadian-style bacon, cut into strips (2 ounces)
- 2 plum-shaped tomatoes, sliced
- ¼ cup crumbled feta cheese (1 ounce)
- 1 green onion, thinly sliced
- 2 teaspoons snipped fresh oregano or basil

Drain artichoke hearts, reserving marinade. Halve artichoke hearts lengthwise; set aside.

Brush the bread shells with some of the reserved marinade. Sprinkle fontina cheese over shells. Divide artichoke hearts, Canadian-style bacon, tomatoes, feta cheese, green onion, and oregano among shells.

Transfer the bread shells to a large piece of double-thickness foil. In a grill with a cover place foil with bread shells on the rack directly over medium heat. Cover and grill about 8 minutes or until cheese is melted and pizza is heated through.

Nutrition facts per serving: 465 cal., 19 g total fat (6 g sat. fat), 44 mg chol., 1,264 mg sodium, 56 g carbo., 2 g fiber, 23 g pro. Daily values: 13% vit. A, 34% vit. C, 24% calcium, 19% iron

# teriyaki pork salad

**In Japanese *teri* means glazed and *yaki* means baked or broiled. The sugar in the marinade caramelizes as it is grilled, giving the pork a beautiful shine. Serve it over mixed greens with peppery radishes, a tasty contrast to the sweetness of the sauce.**



- **4 boneless pork top loin chops, cut ¾ inch thick**
- **⅓ cup rice vinegar**
- **⅓ cup orange juice**
- **2 tablespoons reduced-sodium teriyaki sauce**
- **1 tablespoon peanut oil or salad oil**
- **1 teaspoon sesame seed, toasted**
- **1 teaspoon bottled minced garlic**
- **6 cups packaged torn mixed salad greens**
- **¾ cup sliced red radishes**
- **¼ cup thinly sliced green onions**

**Prep: 15 minutes Marinate: 20 minutes Grill: 8 minutes**
**Makes 4 servings**

Trim fat from chops. Place chops in a plastic bag set in a shallow dish. For marinade, whisk together vinegar, orange juice, teriyaki sauce, oil, sesame seed, and garlic. Reserve half for dressing. Pour the remaining marinade over the chops; close bag. Marinate in refrigerator at least 20 minutes or up to 8 hours, turning bag occasionally.

Drain chops, reserving marinade. Grill the chops on the rack of an uncovered grill directly over medium heat for 8 to 11 minutes or until chops are slightly pink in center and the juices run clear, turning and brushing once with marinade halfway through grilling. Discard any remaining marinade.

Divide greens, radishes, and green onions among 4 dinner plates. Thinly slice pork diagonally and arrange on top of greens. Drizzle with dressing.

Nutrition facts per serving: 199 cal., 11 g total fat (3 g sat. fat), 51 mg chol., 172 mg sodium, 7 g carbo., 1 g fiber, 18 g pro. Daily values: 4% vit. A, 28% vit. C, 2% calcium, 8% iron

# peach-mustard glazed ham

**Head south to a sunnier clime at dinnertime. Fresh peaches and ham—two Southern specialties—make perfect partners in this sweet and smoky dish. Serve it with warm cornbread spread with butter and honey.**



**Prep: 5 minutes Grill: 12 minutes**
**Makes 4 servings**

- 2 tablespoons brown sugar
- 2 tablespoons spicy brown mustard
- ⅓ cup peach or apricot nectar
- 1 1-pound cooked ham slice, cut ¾ to 1 inch thick
- 4 medium peaches, peeled and halved lengthwise
- 2 small green and/or red sweet peppers, each cut crosswise into 4 rings

For glaze, in a bowl combine brown sugar and mustard. Gradually whisk in nectar until smooth. To prevent ham from curling, make shallow cuts around the edge at 1-inch intervals. Brush one side of ham with glaze. Grill ham, glazed-side down, on the greased rack of an uncovered grill directly over medium-hot heat for 6 minutes. Turn ham. Add peaches and peppers. Brush ham, peaches, and peppers with glaze. Grill for 6 to 10 minutes or until heated through, brushing occasionally with glaze.

Nutrition facts per serving: 284 cal., 7 g total fat (2 g sat. fat), 60 mg chol., 1,468 mg sodium, 31 g carbo., 3 g fiber, 26 g pro. Daily values: 11% vit. A, 94% vit. C, 2% calcium, 15% iron

## fired up about smoking (on the grill)

You don't need a smoker to smoke meats. Adding wood chips or chunks to your briquettes gives grilled foods a special wood-smoked aroma and flavor. Good wood-chip choices include mesquite, alder, hickory, oak, and fruitwoods such as apple, cherry, and peach. Read the package labels; it's likely you'll need to soak the chips before you use them so they'll smoke—not burn. If you have a gas grill, try charcoal-flavored briquettes made specifically for gas grills. The hardwoods they contain—such as mesquite and hickory—impart a wood-smoked taste and aroma to grilled foods.

# jamaican pork chops with melon salsa

**The jerk cooks of Jamaica may use dry rubs or wet marinades but the central ingredient in all jerk seasoning is allspice (along with fiery Scotch bonnet chilies and thyme), which grows in abundance on the sunny island.**



- 1 cup chopped honeydew melon
- 1 cup chopped cantaloupe
- 1 tablespoon snipped fresh mint
- 1 tablespoon honey
- 4 boneless pork top loin chops, cut ¾ to 1 inch thick
- 4 teaspoons Jamaican jerk seasoning
- Fresh mint and/or star anise (optional)

Prep: 15 minutes Grill: 8 minutes
Makes 4 servings

For salsa, in a bowl combine honeydew, cantaloupe, the 1 tablespoon mint, and the honey. Cover and refrigerate until ready to serve.

Trim fat from chops. Rub both sides of the chops with Jamaican jerk seasoning. Grill chops on the rack of an uncovered grill directly over medium heat for 8 to 12 minutes or until the chops are slightly pink in center and juices run clear. Serve salsa with chops. If desired, garnish with star anise or additional mint.

Nutrition facts per serving: 189 cal., 8 g total fat (3 g sat. fat), 51 mg chol., 231 mg sodium, 13 g carbo., 1 g fiber, 17 g pro. Daily values: 22% vit. A, 48% vit. C, 2% calcium, 10% iron

# lamb burgers with feta & mint

**Hold the catsup and mustard! You won't need either on these decidedly different burgers. The tang of feta cheese and the refreshing flavor of fresh mint enliven these peppered lamb (or beef) burgers.**



- **1 pound lean ground lamb or beef**
- **2 teaspoons freshly ground pepper**
- **4 lettuce leaves**
- **4 kaiser rolls, split**
- **½ cup crumbled feta cheese (2 ounces)**
- **4 tomato slices**
- **1 tablespoon snipped fresh mint**

**Prep: 15 minutes Grill: 14 minutes**
**Makes 4 servings**

Form ground lamb into four ¾-inch-thick patties. Press pepper evenly into patties. Grill patties on the greased rack of an uncovered grill directly over medium heat for 14 to 18 minutes or until meat is no longer pink, turning once.

Place lettuce on bottoms of rolls. Top with patties, feta cheese, tomato slices, and mint.

Nutrition facts per serving: 435 cal., 21 g total fat (9 g sat. fat), 88 mg chol., 535 mg sodium, 33 g carbo., 1 g fiber, 28 g pro. Daily values: 4% vit. A, 11% vit. C, 12% calcium, 27% iron

## is it **done** yet?

Because of the high temperature of the grill, meats can cook quickly on the outside—in fact, they can burn—before the inside is done. You can determine doneness of steaks by making a small slit near the bone and checking for color. For boneless steaks, make a slit near the center. Ground-meat patties with no other added ingredients should be cooked at least until the centers are brownish pink (medium doneness). Ground-meat patties with added ingredients—eggs, bread crumbs, onions, or liquid—should be cooked to 170° or until no pink remains. Cut into the patty to see that the color of the center of the patty is brown.

# greek-inspired lamb pockets

**Be a dinnertime hero with a meal-in-a-pocket that will win you applause. Meaty lamb leg or shoulder is marinated in balsamic vinegar, pepper, and fresh herbs, quick-grilled to keep it juicy, then tucked into a pita and topped with a creamy yogurt sauce.**



**Prep: 20 minutes Marinate: 10 minutes Grill: 10 minutes**
**Makes 4 servings**

- **1 pound boneless lamb leg or shoulder**
- **¼ cup balsamic vinegar**
- **1 tablespoon snipped fresh savory or 1 teaspoon dried savory, crushed**
- **½ teaspoon pepper**
- **1 8-ounce carton plain low-fat or fat-free yogurt**
- **1 small cucumber, peeled, seeded, and chopped (¾ cup)**
- **2 plum-shaped tomatoes, chopped**
- **1 small onion, finely chopped**
- **4 whole wheat pita bread rounds**

Trim fat from lamb. Cut lamb into 2×1-inch thin strips. Place lamb in a plastic bag set in a shallow dish. For marinade, combine the vinegar, savory, and pepper. Pour marinade over lamb; close bag. Marinate in the refrigerator at least 10 minutes or up to 4 hours, turning bag once. Meanwhile, for sauce, in a medium bowl combine yogurt, cucumber, tomatoes, and onion. Cover and refrigerate until ready to serve. Wrap pita rounds in foil. Set aside.

Drain lamb, reserving marinade. On four 12-inch skewers thread lamb, accordion-style. Grill kabobs on the rack of an uncovered grill directly over medium heat for 10 to 12 minutes or to desired doneness, turning kabobs once and brushing occasionally with marinade up to the last 5 minutes. Place the pita rounds on grill rack next to the kabobs the last 5 minutes of grilling. Discard any remaining marinade.

Cut pita rounds in half crosswise. Spoon the sauce into pita halves and fill with lamb strips.

Nutrition facts per serving: 361 cal., 8 g total fat (3 g sat. fat), 61 mg chol., 430 mg sodium, 46 g carbo., 1 g fiber, 28 g pro. Daily values: 3% vit. A, 20% vit. C, 10% calcium, 15% iron

# apple-glazed lamb chops

**Lamb chops make an elegant quick-to-fix dish, and these cinnamon- and apple-spiced lamb chops are the ultimate company fare. Add a side of couscous tossed with fresh mint and finish with a scoop of sorbet for a weekday dinner with friends.**



**Prep: 15 minutes Grill: 14 minutes**
**Makes 4 servings**

- **3 tablespoons apple jelly**
- **1 green onion, thinly sliced**
- **1 tablespoon soy sauce**
- **2 teaspoons lemon juice**
- **⅛ teaspoon curry powder**
- **Dash ground cinnamon**
- **Dash ground red pepper**
- **2 small red and/or green apples, cut crosswise into ¼-inch-thick slices**
- **Lemon juice**
- **8 lamb loin chops, cut 1 inch thick**
- **Hot cooked couscous (optional)**
- **1 tablespoon snipped fresh mint**

For glaze, in a small saucepan heat and stir apple jelly, green onion, soy sauce, lemon juice, curry powder, cinnamon, and red pepper over medium heat until bubbly. Remove from heat. Remove seeds from apple slices. Brush apples with lemon juice. Set aside.

Trim fat from chops. Grill chops on the rack of an uncovered grill directly over medium heat until chops are cooked to desired doneness, turning and brushing once with glaze. (Allow 10 to 14 minutes for medium-rare and 14 to 16 minutes for medium doneness.) Place apples on grill rack next to chops the last 5 minutes of grilling, turning and brushing once with glaze.

If desired, serve chops and apples with couscous. Sprinkle with mint.

Nutrition facts per serving: 385 cal., 14 g total fat (5 g sat. fat), 133 mg chol., 378 mg sodium, 20 g carbo., 1 g fiber, 43 g pro. Daily values: 1% vit. A, 11% vit. C, 3% calcium, 23% iron

# so easy seafood

# salmon with fresh pineapple salsa

**You don't need to have a party—just a weeknight dinner will do—to enjoy the sweet-hot fruit salsa that's as pretty as a sprinkling of confetti on top of this grilled salmon fillet. Serve it with hot cooked rice.**



**Start to finish: 30 minutes**
**Makes 4 servings**

- **2 cups coarsely chopped fresh pineapple**
- **½ cup chopped red sweet pepper**
- **¼ cup finely chopped red onion**
- **3 tablespoons lime juice**
- **1 small fresh jalapeño pepper, seeded and finely chopped**
- **1 tablespoon snipped fresh cilantro or chives**
- **1 tablespoon honey**
- **1 1-pound fresh skinless salmon fillet, 1 inch thick**
- **¼ teaspoon ground cumin**

For salsa, in a medium bowl combine pineapple, sweet pepper, onion, 2 tablespoons of the lime juice, the jalapeño pepper, cilantro, and honey. Set aside.

Rinse fish; pat dry. Brush both sides of fish with the remaining lime juice and sprinkle with cumin. Place fish in a well-greased wire grill basket. Grill fish on the rack of an uncovered grill directly over medium heat for 8 to 12 minutes or until fish flakes easily with a fork, turning basket once. Cut fish into 4 serving-size pieces. Serve with the salsa.

Nutrition facts per serving: 170 cal., 4 g total fat (1 g sat. fat), 20 mg chol., 70 mg sodium, 17 g carbo., 1 g fiber, 17 g pro. Daily values: 16% vit. A, 75% vit. C, 1% calcium, 9% iron

# salmon with cucumber kabobs

**Cooked cucumbers provide a pleasant change of pace on these kabobs. Though their characteristic crispness disappears with cooking, their delicacy does not, making them a perfect companion for light and elegant fish dishes.**



- **4 6- to 8-ounce fresh skinless salmon fillets, ½ to 1 inch thick**
- **⅓ cup lemon juice**
- **1 tablespoon olive oil or cooking oil**
- **2 teaspoons snipped fresh tarragon**
- **1 medium cucumber, halved lengthwise and sliced 1 inch thick**
- **1 medium red onion, cut into wedges**
- **8 cherry tomatoes**
- **Hot cooked rice (optional)**

**Prep: 15 minutes Marinate: 10 minutes Grill: 8 minutes**
**Makes 4 servings**

Rinse fish; pat dry. Place fish in a plastic bag set in a shallow dish. For marinade, combine lemon juice, oil, and tarragon. Reserve half for basting. Pour remaining marinade over fish; close bag. Marinate at room temperature for 10 to 20 minutes. Meanwhile, on four 10-inch skewers alternately thread cucumber and onion.

Drain fish, discarding marinade. Place fish in a well-greased wire grill basket. Grill the fish and vegetables on the rack of an uncovered grill directly over medium heat until fish flakes easily with a fork and vegetables are tender, turning basket and vegetables once and brushing occasionally with basting sauce. (Allow 4 to 6 minutes per ½-inch thickness of fish and 8 to 12 minutes for vegetables.) Add tomatoes to ends of kabobs the last 2 minutes of grilling.

If desired, serve fish and vegetables with rice.

Nutrition facts per serving: 201 cal., 8 g total fat (2 g sat. fat), 31 mg chol., 106 mg sodium, 6 g carbo., 1 g fiber, 25 g pro. Daily values: 6% vit. A, 25% vit. C, 2% calcium, 9% iron

# panzanella with grilled tuna

**Pané means bread in Italian, and making panzanella is a wonderful way to use bread that's not as fresh as just-baked but still too good to throw away. Bread salad may be an economical way to use up leftover bread, but it's simply delicious, too.**



**Prep: 20 minutes Grill: 4 minutes Stand: 5 minutes**
**Makes 4 servings**

- ½ cup bottled balsamic vinaigrette or red wine vinegar salad dressing
- ½ teaspoon finely snipped fresh rosemary
- 1 pound fresh tuna steaks, ½ to 1 inch thick
- 2 cups packaged torn mixed salad greens
- 1½ cups broccoli flowerets
- 2 small tomatoes, chopped
- ¼ cup thinly sliced green onions
- 4 cups 1-inch cubes day-old Italian bread
- Finely shredded Parmesan cheese (optional)

For sauce, in a small bowl combine vinaigrette and rosemary. Reserve 2 tablespoons for dressing.

Rinse fish; pat dry. Grill fish on the greased rack of an uncovered grill directly over medium heat until fish flakes easily with a fork, turning and brushing once with remaining sauce. (Allow 4 to 6 minutes per ½-inch thickness of fish.)

Meanwhile, in a large salad bowl combine greens, broccoli, tomatoes, and green onions. Flake fish; add to greens mixture. Drizzle with the dressing; toss gently to coat. Add bread cubes; toss gently to combine. Let stand for 5 minutes before serving. If desired, sprinkle with cheese.

Nutrition facts per serving: 380 cal., 17 g total fat (3 g sat. fat), 47 mg chol., 608 mg sodium, 24 g carbo., 2 g fiber, 33 g pro. Daily values: 82% vit. A, 69% vit. C, 5% calcium, 19% iron

# shark with nectarine salsa

**Shark usually is sold as fillets, but if you can't find it, orange roughy makes a fine substitute. Orange roughy, found in the waters near New Zealand and Australia, has firm white flesh with a mild flavor. However, any mild white fish is acceptable.**



**Prep: 30 minutes Grill: 8 minutes**
**Makes 4 servings**

For salsa, in a bowl combine nectarine, cucumber, kiwi fruit, onions, orange juice, and vinegar. Cover and refrigerate until ready to serve.

Rinse fish; pat dry. Rub oil over both sides of fish and sprinkle with pepper. Place fish in a well-greased wire grill basket. Grill fish on the rack of an uncovered grill directly over medium heat for 8 to 12 minutes or until fish flakes easily with a fork, turning basket once. Spoon the salsa over fish. Cut fish into 4 serving-size pieces.

Nutrition facts per serving: 158 cal., 3 g total fat (1 g sat. fat), 60 mg chol., 94 mg sodium, 10 g carbo., 1 g fiber, 22 g pro. Daily values: 6% vit. A, 55% vit. C, 3% calcium, 5% iron

**1** **ripe nectarine, cut into ½-inch pieces**

**1** **small cucumber, seeded and cut into ½-inch pieces**

**1** **ripe kiwi fruit, peeled and cut into ½-inch pieces**

**¼** **cup thinly sliced green onions**

**3** **tablespoons orange juice**

**1** **tablespoon white wine vinegar**

**1** **1-pound fresh shark or orange roughy fillet, 1 inch thick**

**1** **teaspoon olive oil**

**½** **teaspoon freshly ground pepper**

## tips for grilling fish

Much of the appeal of fish is that it is so tender and delicate. Fish is a great candidate for the grill—with a little extra care to prevent it from breaking apart. It helps to place fish on foil (and use a wide spatula if you must turn it) or in a grill basket when grilling. Grill baskets are intended for direct grilling only—most grill-basket handles can't take the heat of indirect cooking on a covered grill. Be sure to lightly grease or brush the foil or basket with cooking oil before adding the fish. Firmer-textured fish steaks can be grilled on a greased grill rack.

# grouper with red pepper sauce

**When you're in the mood for fish, look to this member of the sea bass family with its mild, sweet flavor. Gild the lily with this exceptional red pepper-tomato sauce.**



- **1 large red sweet pepper, chopped**
- **1 tablespoon margarine or butter**
- **2 medium tomatoes, peeled, seeded, and chopped**
- **1 tablespoon sugar**
- **1 teaspoon red wine vinegar**
- **¼ teaspoon salt**
- **⅛ teaspoon garlic powder**
- **Dash ground red pepper**
- **2 tablespoons lemon juice**
- **1 tablespoon olive oil**
- **¼ teaspoon dried rosemary, crushed**
- **4 4-ounce fresh grouper fillets, ½ to 1 inch thick**

**Prep: 25 minutes Grill: 4 minutes**
**Makes 4 servings**

For sauce, in a medium saucepan cook sweet pepper in hot margarine or butter over medium heat until tender. Stir in tomatoes, sugar, vinegar, salt, garlic powder, and ground red pepper. Cook for 5 minutes, stirring occasionally. Transfer mixture to a blender container or food processor bowl. Cover and blend or process until smooth. Return to saucepan; cover and keep warm.*

In a small bowl combine the lemon juice, oil, and rosemary. Rinse fish; pat dry. Brush both sides of fish with lemon mixture. Place fish in a well-greased wire grill basket. Grill fish on the rack of an uncovered grill directly over medium heat until fish flakes easily with a fork, turning basket once. (Allow 4 to 6 minutes per ½-inch thickness of fish.) Serve sauce with fish.

Nutrition facts per serving: 194 cal., 8 g total fat (1 g sat. fat), 60 mg chol., 266 mg sodium, 9 g carbo., 1 g fiber, 22 g pro. Daily values: 27% vit. A, 97% vit. C, 2% calcium, 5% iron

**Note: If desired, you may prepare the sauce ahead of time and refrigerate until ready to grill. Before serving, reheat the sauce in a saucepan.*

# blackened catfish with roasted potatoes

**Catch a pan-fried Cajun classic and cook it on your grill! This version of a Southern favorite is served alongside tiny new potatoes, carrots, and onions roasted in olive oil and zippy hot pepper sauce.**



**Prep: 20 minutes  Grill: 35 minutes**
**Makes 4 servings**

- 1 tablespoon olive oil
- ¼ teaspoon salt
- Several dashes bottled hot pepper sauce
- 1½ pounds tiny new potatoes, thinly sliced
- 4 medium carrots, thinly sliced
- 1 medium green sweet pepper, cut into thin strips
- 1 medium onion, sliced
- 4 4- to 5-ounce fresh or frozen catfish or red snapper fillets, ½ to 1 inch thick
- ½ teaspoon Cajun seasoning
- Nonstick spray coating
- 1 tablespoon snipped fresh chervil or parsley

Fold a 48×18-inch piece of heavy foil in half to make a 24×18-inch rectangle. In a large bowl combine the oil, salt, and pepper sauce. Add the potatoes, carrots, sweet pepper, and onion; toss to coat. Place in the center of foil. Bring up 2 opposite edges of foil; seal with a double fold. Fold remaining ends to completely enclose vegetables, leaving space for steam to build.

Grill vegetables on the rack of an uncovered grill directly over medium heat for 35 to 40 minutes or until potatoes and carrots are tender.

Meanwhile, thaw fish, if frozen. Rinse fish; pat dry. Sprinkle both sides of fish with Cajun seasoning and lightly spray with nonstick coating. Place fish in a well-greased wire grill basket. While the vegetables cook, place the fish on the grill rack next to the vegetables and grill until fish flakes easily with a fork, turning the basket once. (Allow 4 to 6 minutes per ½-inch thickness of fish.) To serve, sprinkle fish and vegetables with snipped chervil.

Nutrition facts per serving: 352 cal., 6 g total fat (1 g sat. fat), 42 mg chol., 266 mg sodium, 48 g carbo., 5 g fiber, 28 g pro. Daily values: 173% vit. A, 63% vit. C, 7% calcium, 24% iron

# thai-spiced scallops

**In addition to the salty, sweet, sour, and spicy flavors that spark Thai cooking, this dish features one more: basil, with its peppery, clovelike flavor—and lots of it. These delicious scallops let you sample the whole spectrum of Thai tastes.**



- **1 pound fresh or frozen sea scallops**
- **2 medium yellow summer squash and/or zucchini, quartered lengthwise and sliced ½ inch thick**
- **1½ cups packaged peeled baby carrots**
- **⅔ cup bottled sweet and sour sauce**
- **2 tablespoons snipped fresh basil**
- **1 teaspoon Thai seasoning or five-spice powder**
- **½ teaspoon bottled minced garlic**

**Start to finish: 30 minutes**
**Makes 4 servings**

Thaw scallops, if frozen. Fold a 36×18-inch piece of heavy foil in half to make an 18×18-inch square. Place squash and carrots in center of foil. Sprinkle lightly with salt and pepper. Bring up 2 opposite edges of foil; seal with a double fold. Fold remaining ends to completely enclose the vegetables, leaving space for steam to build. Grill vegetables on the rack of an uncovered grill directly over medium heat for 15 to 20 minutes or until vegetables are crisp-tender, turning vegetables occasionally.

Meanwhile, for the sauce, in a small bowl combine the sweet and sour sauce, basil, Thai seasoning, and garlic. Transfer ¼ cup of the sauce to another bowl for basting. Reserve remaining sauce until ready to serve.

Rinse scallops; pat dry. Halve any large scallops. On four 8- to 10-inch skewers thread scallops. Place kabobs on grill rack next to vegetables the last 5 to 8 minutes of grilling or until scallops are opaque, turning and brushing once with basting sauce. Serve scallops and vegetables with the remaining sauce.

Nutrition facts per serving: 168 cal., 1 g total fat (0 g sat. fat), 34 mg chol., 370 mg sodium, 25 g carbo., 3 g fiber, 16 g pro. Daily values: 122% vit. A, 17% vit. C, 9% calcium, 18% iron

# pepper shrimp in peanut sauce

**Who could resist this dish? Sweet and spicy peanut sauce dresses up whimsical bow-tie pasta, colorful and crisp sweet peppers, and best of all, the special treat of grilled shrimp.**



- **1 pound fresh or frozen medium shrimp in shells**
- **8 ounces dried bow-tie pasta or linguine**
- **½ cup water**
- **¼ cup orange marmalade**
- **2 tablespoons peanut butter**
- **2 tablespoons soy sauce**
- **2 teaspoons cornstarch**
- **¼ teaspoon crushed red pepper**
- **2 medium red, yellow, and/or green sweet peppers, cut into 1-inch pieces**
- **Chopped peanuts (optional)**

**Start to finish: 35 minutes**
**Makes 4 servings**

Thaw shrimp, if frozen. Peel and devein shrimp, leaving tails intact. Rinse shrimp; pat dry. Set aside. Cook the pasta according to package directions. Drain. Return pasta to pan; keep warm.

Meanwhile, for sauce, in a small saucepan stir together the water, orange marmalade, peanut butter, soy sauce, cornstarch, and crushed red pepper. Bring to boiling; reduce heat. Cook and stir for 2 minutes. Remove from heat and keep warm.

On eight 12-inch skewers alternately thread shrimp and sweet peppers. Grill kabobs on the rack of an uncovered grill directly over medium heat for 6 to 8 minutes or until shrimp turn pink, turning once.

To serve, add shrimp and peppers to the cooked pasta. Add the sauce; toss gently to coat. If desired, sprinkle individual servings with peanuts.

Nutrition facts per serving: 382 cal., 7 g total fat (1 g sat. fat), 180 mg chol., 718 mg sodium, 57 g carbo., 3 g fiber, 24 g pro. Daily values: 34% vit. A, 108% vit. C, 4% calcium, 33% iron

# asparagus & shrimp with dill butter

**This lovely dish is the essence of spring (leeks, asparagus, fresh dill) and the essence of elegance (a touch of white wine and butter) in one. It's simple enough for weeknight dining but special enough to serve guests.**



**Prep: 20 minutes  Grill: 15 minutes**
**Makes 4 servings**

- 1 pound fresh or frozen medium shrimp in shells
- 1 pound asparagus spears
- ¼ cup butter or margarine, softened
- 1 tablespoon snipped fresh dill or 1 teaspoon dried dillweed
- 1 tablespoon dry white wine
- ½ teaspoon finely shredded lemon peel
- ⅛ teaspoon salt
- ⅛ teaspoon pepper
- 1 medium leek, thinly sliced
- 3 cups hot cooked rice or pasta

Thaw shrimp, if frozen. Peel and devein shrimp, removing tails, if desired. Rinse shrimp; pat dry. Snap off and discard woody bases from asparagus. Bias-slice the asparagus into 2-inch pieces. In a bowl stir together the butter or margarine, dill, wine, lemon peel, salt, and pepper. Set aside.

Fold a 36×18-inch piece of heavy foil in half to make an 18×18-inch square. Place shrimp, asparagus, and leek in center of foil. Top with dill mixture. Bring up 2 opposite edges of foil; seal with a double fold. Fold remaining ends to completely enclose shrimp mixture, leaving space for steam to build.

Grill foil packet on the rack of an uncovered grill directly over medium heat about 15 minutes or until shrimp turn pink, turning packet once.

Serve the shrimp and vegetables over rice. Drizzle with the juices from foil packet.

Nutrition facts per serving: 350 cal., 13 g total fat (2 g sat. fat), 131 mg chol., 357 mg sodium, 39 g carbo., 2 g fiber, 19 g pro. Daily values: 25% vit. A, 35% vit. C, 5% calcium, 28% iron

# shrimp & tropical fruit

**Fruit cocktail goes uptown! With the addition of sweet and savory barbecued shrimp, a fresh-fruit salad of pineapple, papaya, and kiwi becomes a whole meal that hints at the warmth, sun, and fun of a tropical isle.**



- 1¼ pounds fresh or frozen jumbo shrimp in shells
- 1 cup bottled barbecue sauce
- ⅔ cup unsweetened pineapple juice
- 2 tablespoons cooking oil
- 4 teaspoons grated gingerroot or 1½ teaspoons ground ginger
- ¼ of a fresh pineapple, sliced crosswise
- 1 medium papaya, peeled, seeded, and cut up
- 3 medium kiwi fruit, peeled and cut up

**Prep: 25 minutes Grill: 10 minutes**
**Makes 6 servings**

Thaw shrimp, if frozen. Peel and devein shrimp, leaving tails intact. Rinse shrimp; pat dry. On six 10- to 12-inch skewers thread shrimp. For sauce, in a medium bowl stir together barbecue sauce, pineapple juice, oil, and gingerroot. Brush shrimp with sauce.

Grill shrimp on the greased rack of an uncovered grill directly over medium heat for 10 to 12 minutes or until shrimp turn pink, turning once and brushing occasionally with sauce. Place pineapple on grill rack next to shrimp the last 5 minutes of grilling, turning once.

Serve shrimp and pineapple with papaya and kiwi fruit. In a small saucepan heat remaining sauce to boiling; cool slightly. Pass for dipping.

Nutrition facts per serving: 199 cal., 6 g total fat (1 g sat. fat), 116 mg chol., 474 mg sodium, 21 g carbo., 1 g fiber, 14 g pro. Daily values: 13% vit. A, 115% vit. C, 5% calcium, 17% iron

vibrant
vegetables

# vegetable kabobs

**These crisp-tender vegetable kabobs are the essence of simplicity—a swath of rosemary-scented oil-and-vinegar dressing is their only embellishment. Threaded onto rosemary stalks, the colorful components look like jewels on a string.**



**Prep: 20 minutes Grill: 10 minutes**
**Makes 4 servings**

- 8 tiny new potatoes, quartered
- 2 tablespoons water
- 8 baby sunburst squash
- 4 miniature sweet peppers and/or 1 red sweet pepper, cut into 1-inch pieces
- 8 tiny red onions, halved, or 2 small red onions, each cut into 8 wedges
- 8 baby zucchini or 1 small zucchini, halved lengthwise and sliced
- ¼ cup bottled oil-and-vinegar salad dressing
- 2 teaspoons snipped fresh rosemary or ½ teaspoon dried rosemary, crushed
- Fresh rosemary (optional)

In a 2-quart microwave-safe casserole combine potatoes and water. Micro-cook, covered, on 100% power (high) for 5 minutes. Gently stir in sunburst squash, sweet peppers, and onions. Cook, covered, on high for 4 to 6 minutes or until nearly tender. Drain. Cool slightly.

On eight 10-inch skewers* alternately thread the sunburst squash, sweet peppers, onions, and zucchini. In a small bowl combine dressing and the 2 teaspoons fresh or ½ teaspoon dried rosemary; brush over vegetables.

Grill kabobs on the rack of an uncovered grill directly over medium heat for 10 to 12 minutes or until vegetables are tender and browned, turning and brushing occasionally with dressing mixture. If desired, garnish with additional fresh rosemary.

Nutrition facts per serving: 161 cal., 8 g total fat (1 g sat. fat), 0 mg chol., 217 mg sodium, 22 g carbo., 2 g fiber, 3 g pro. Daily values: 15% vit. A, 75% vit. C, 2% calcium, 7% iron

**Note: Using rosemary skewers will add a special touch to your meal. To use fresh rosemary skewers, first grill the vegetables on regular metal skewers (the rosemary will burn if grilled), then thread grilled vegetables on long stalks of fresh rosemary, removing some of the rosemary leaves.*

# eggplant with gorgonzola

**The mild, sweet taste and meaty texture of eggplant lends itself especially well to grilling. This lovely combination of glossy purple eggplant, yellow summer squash, and red onion is the perfect accompaniment to grilled chicken.**



- 1 small eggplant (about 12 ounces)
- 1 medium yellow summer squash, halved lengthwise and sliced 1 inch thick
- 1 small red onion, cut into thin wedges
- 2 tablespoons pesto
- ¼ cup crumbled Gorgonzola or other blue cheese, feta cheese, or goat (chèvre) cheese (1 ounce)

**Prep: 10 minutes Grill: 20 minutes**
**Makes 4 servings**

If desired, peel eggplant. Cut into 1-inch cubes. In a large bowl combine the eggplant, squash, onion, and pesto; toss gently to coat. Fold a 36×18-inch piece of heavy foil in half to make an 18×18-inch square. Place vegetables in center of foil. Bring up 2 opposite edges of foil; seal with a double fold. Fold the remaining ends to completely enclose the vegetables, leaving space for steam to build.*

Grill vegetables on the rack of an uncovered grill directly over medium heat for 20 to 25 minutes or until vegetables are crisp-tender, turning them occasionally.

To serve, transfer vegetables to a serving bowl and sprinkle with cheese.

Nutrition facts per serving: 116 cal., 8 g total fat (2 g sat. fat), 7 mg chol., 179 mg sodium, 9 g carbo., 3 g fiber, 4 g pro. Daily values: 3% vit. A, 5% vit. C, 4% calcium, 2% iron

**Note: If desired, you may assemble the foil packet ahead of time and refrigerate until ready to grill. Add a few minutes to the grilling time.*

# peppers stuffed with goat cheese

**Stuffed peppers just got lighter and more elegant! These easy-to-make sweet peppers filled with creamy, tangy goat cheese and loads of fresh herbs make impressive, yet quick, company fare that will complement a grilled steak and a hearty glass of wine.**



**Prep: 15 minutes  Grill: 5 minutes**
**Makes 4 servings**

- **2** medium red, yellow, or green sweet peppers, halved lengthwise
- **1** ounce soft goat (chèvre) cheese
- **¼** cup shredded Monterey Jack cheese (1 ounce)
- **1** tablespoon snipped fresh chives
- **1** tablespoon snipped fresh basil or 1 teaspoon dried basil, crushed

In a medium covered saucepan cook peppers in a small amount of boiling water for 2 minutes. Drain, cut sides down, on paper towels.

Meanwhile, for cheese mixture, in a small bowl combine goat cheese, Monterey Jack cheese, chives, and basil. Spoon into pepper shells.

Fold a 24×18-inch piece of heavy foil in half to make a 12×18-inch rectangle. Place peppers in center of foil. Bring up 2 opposite edges of foil; seal with a double fold. Fold remaining ends to completely enclose peppers, leaving space for steam to build.

Grill peppers on the rack of an uncovered grill directly over medium to medium-hot heat for 5 to 6 minutes or until peppers are crisp-tender and cheese is melted.

Nutrition facts per serving: 60 cal., 4 g total fat (2 g sat. fat), 13 mg chol., 80 mg sodium, 3 g carbo., 0 g fiber, 3 g pro. Daily values: 30% vit. A, 104% vit. C, 4% calcium

# grilled tomatoes with pesto

**They say there are two things money can't buy: love and homegrown tomatoes. If you don't have the latter, search out a farmer's market for the makings of this summer dish. It will garner you love from all who are lucky enough to taste it.**



**Prep: 15 minutes Grill: 15 minutes**
**Makes 6 servings**

- **3 to 5 small to medium red, orange, and/or yellow tomatoes, cored and halved crosswise**
- **2 tablespoons pesto**
- **6 very thin onion slices**
- **½ cup shredded Monterey Jack cheese (2 ounces)**
- **⅓ cup smoky-flavored whole almonds, chopped**
- **2 tablespoons snipped fresh parsley**

Using a spoon, hollow out the top ¼ inch of tomato halves. Top with pesto, then onion slices. Place tomatoes in a foil pie plate.

In a grill with a cover arrange preheated coals around edge of grill. Test for medium heat in center of the grill. Place the tomatoes in center of grill rack. Cover and grill for 10 to 15 minutes or until tomatoes are heated through.

Meanwhile, in a small bowl stir together cheese, almonds, and parsley. Sprinkle over tomatoes. Cover and grill about 5 minutes more or until cheese is melted. Sprinkle lightly with salt and pepper.

Nutrition facts per serving: 132 cal., 10 g total fat (2 g sat. fat), 9 mg chol., 119 mg sodium, 6 g carbo., 2 g fiber, 5 g pro. Daily values: 7% vit. A, 24% vit. C, 8% calcium, 5% iron

# summer squash with cheese & sage

**The smaller the squash you choose, the sweeter they are likely to be. As the squash cook, their natural sugar caramelizes—giving them a nutty, rich flavor. They soak up a wonderful, smoky flavor, too—a terrific combination with the salty tang of goat cheese.**



- **1 pound small yellow summer squash or zucchini**
- **1 teaspoon olive oil**
- **¼ cup mild picante sauce**
- **2 tablespoons crumbled goat (chèvre) cheese or shredded Monterey Jack cheese**
- **1 tablespoon snipped fresh sage, oregano, or cilantro**

**Prep: 5 minutes Grill: 10 minutes**
**Makes 4 servings**

Trim ends from squash; halve squash lengthwise. In a medium bowl combine squash and oil; toss gently to coat.

Grill squash, cut sides down, on the greased rack of an uncovered grill directly over medium heat about 10 minutes or until squash are crisp-tender, turning once and brushing occasionally with picante sauce. Transfer squash to a serving bowl and sprinkle with cheese and sage.

Nutrition facts per serving: 54 cal., 4 g total fat (1 g sat. fat), 7 mg chol., 156 mg sodium, 5 g carbo., 1 g fiber, 2 g pro. Daily values: 4% vit. A, 14% vit. C, 1% calcium, 3% iron

## fresh-herb interchanges

Fresh herbs turn ordinary dishes into extraordinary ones. Herbs each have their own distinct flavors, but you can have one step in for another. Try these substitutions:

- Sage: use savory, marjoram, or rosemary
- Basil: substitute oregano or thyme
- Thyme: basil, marjoram, oregano, or savory will suffice
- Mint: substitute basil, marjoram, or rosemary
- Rosemary: try thyme, tarragon, or savory
- Cilantro: substitute parsley

# summer squash combo

**This humble squash gets a French accent with deeply flavored walnut oil—a Gallic favorite. Walnut oil is delicate and should be refrigerated. If the oil becomes cloudy and solid, let it stand several minutes at room temperature before using.**



**Prep: 15 minutes Grill: 5 minutes**
**Makes 4 to 6 servings**

- 2 tablespoons walnut oil or olive oil
- 1 tablespoon olive oil
- 2 teaspoons snipped fresh rosemary or ½ teaspoon dried rosemary, crushed
- ½ teaspoon salt
- ½ to 1 teaspoon crushed red pepper
- ½ teaspoon bottled minced garlic
- 2 medium red onions, cut crosswise into ¾-inch-thick slices
- 2 medium zucchini, cut lengthwise into quarters
- 2 medium yellow summer squash, cut lengthwise into quarters

In a small bowl stir together walnut oil, the 1 tablespoon olive oil, the rosemary, salt, red pepper, and garlic. Brush the onions, zucchini, and yellow squash with some of the oil mixture.

Grill vegetables on the rack of an uncovered grill directly over medium to medium-hot heat for 5 to 6 minutes or until crisp-tender and lightly browned, turning and brushing once with remaining oil mixture.

Nutrition facts per serving: 126 cal., 10 g total fat (1 g sat. fat), 0 mg chol., 272 mg sodium, 8 g carbo., 2 g fiber, 1 g pro. Daily values: 4% vit. A, 12% vit. C, 2% calcium, 3% iron

# warm tarragon potato salad

**A picnic favorite has been lightened and brightened up with a tangy fresh-herb and Dijon vinaigrette dressing, crunchy bok choy, and peppery radishes. Tarragon, with its aniselike flavor, makes a fine complement to mild foods such as potatoes or fish.**



- **¼ cup salad oil**
- **¼ cup vinegar**
- **1 tablespoon sugar (optional)**
- **1 teaspoon snipped fresh tarragon or dill or ¼ teaspoon dried tarragon, crushed, or dried dillweed**
- **½ teaspoon Dijon-style mustard**
- **1 pound tiny new potatoes and/or small yellow potatoes, cut into bite-size pieces**
- **2 teaspoons salad oil**
- **1 cup chopped bok choy**
- **½ cup chopped red radishes**
- **½ cup thinly sliced green onions**
- **2 thin slices Canadian-style bacon, chopped (1 ounce)**
- **⅛ teaspoon freshly ground pepper**
- **4 artichokes, cooked, halved lengthwise, and choke removed (optional)**

**Prep: 10 minutes Grill: 25 minutes**
**Makes 8 servings**

For dressing, in a small bowl whisk together the ¼ cup oil, the vinegar, sugar (if desired), tarragon, and mustard. Set aside.

In a lightly greased 2-quart square foil pan combine potatoes and the 2 teaspoons oil; toss to coat.

In a grill with a cover arrange preheated coals around edge of grill. Test for medium-hot heat in center of grill. Place potatoes in center of grill rack. Cover and grill about 25 minutes or just until potatoes are tender. Cool potatoes slightly.

In a large bowl combine potatoes, bok choy, radishes, green onions, Canadian-style bacon, and pepper. Add the dressing; toss gently to coat. If desired, spoon the salad into artichoke halves.

Nutrition facts per serving: 135 cal., 8 g total fat (1 g sat. fat), 2 mg chol., 68 mg sodium, 14 g carbo., 1 g fiber, 2 g pro. Daily values: 2% vit. A, 21% vit. C, 2% calcium, 7% iron

# grilled asparagus with sorrel dressing

**The essence of lemon brings out the very best in fresh asparagus. Here, the lemony tartness comes from delicate sorrel greens, which are used to flavor the fresh-tasting yogurt-mayonnaise dressing. Look for sorrel especially in the spring.**



- **¼ cup plain low-fat yogurt**
- **¼ cup mayonnaise or salad dressing**
- **¼ cup finely snipped sorrel or spinach**
- **1 green onion, thinly sliced**
- **1 teaspoon lemon-pepper seasoning (optional)**
- **1 pound asparagus spears**
- **2 tablespoons water**

**Prep: 10 minutes Grill: 15 minutes**
**Makes 4 servings**

For dressing, in a small bowl combine yogurt, mayonnaise, sorrel, green onion, and, if desired, lemon-pepper seasoning. Cover and refrigerate until ready to serve.

Fold a 36×18-inch piece of heavy foil in half to make an 18×18-inch square. Snap off and discard the woody bases from asparagus. Place asparagus in center of foil. Fold up edges of foil slightly; drizzle asparagus with water. Bring up 2 opposite edges of foil; seal with a double fold. Fold remaining ends to completely enclose the asparagus, leaving space for steam to build.

Grill asparagus on the rack of an uncovered grill directly over medium-hot heat about 15 minutes or until crisp-tender, turning once. Serve asparagus with the dressing.

Nutrition facts per serving: 129 cal., 11 g total fat (2 g sat. fat), 9 mg chol., 95 mg sodium, 5 g carbo., 2 g fiber, 3 g pro. Daily values: 10% vit. A, 38% vit. C, 4% calcium, 5% iron

# cilantro corn on the cob

**The pleasures of the American summer could be distilled into this: tender, sweet corn on the cob, roasted and bursting with fresh herb flavor. Try substituting fresh basil for the cilantro, if you like—and pass the napkins, please.**



**Prep: 10 minutes Grill: 20 minutes**
**Makes 4 servings**

- **1 tablespoon snipped fresh cilantro**
- **1 tablespoon olive oil**
- **1 to 2 teaspoons crushed red pepper**
- **⅛ teaspoon salt**
- **Dash black pepper**
- **4 fresh ears of corn**

In a bowl combine cilantro, oil, red pepper, salt, and black pepper. Remove husks from corn. Scrub ears with a stiff brush to remove silks. Rinse corn; pat dry. Place each ear of corn on a piece of heavy foil. Brush ears with cilantro mixture. Wrap the corn securely in foil. Grill corn on the rack of an uncovered grill directly over medium to medium-hot heat about 20 minutes or until kernels are tender, turning frequently.

Nutrition facts per serving: 116 cal., 4 g total fat (1 g sat. fat), 0 mg chol., 90 mg sodium, 20 g carbo., 3 g fiber, 3 g pro. Daily values: 8% vit. A, 7% vit. C, 4% iron

## it's hot, hot, hot (or not)

Unless you have a thermometer on your grill, you'll need a good way to measure the approximate temperature of the coals. Here's a simple test: Hold your hand, for as long as it's comfortable, where the food will cook. The number of seconds you can hold it there gives you a clue.

| Number of Seconds | Coal Temperature |
|---|---|
| 2 | High |
| 3 | Medium-high |
| 4 | Medium |
| 5 | Medium-low |
| 6 | Low |

sauces,
marinades,
& rubs

# herb rub

**Here's an aromatic way to flavor grilled meats that doesn't depend on having fresh herbs. Try this rub on steak or chicken.**

**Prep: 5 minutes**
**Makes about 2 teaspoons, enough for 2½ to 3 pounds bone-in chicken (6 servings).**

In a small bowl combine ½ teaspoon salt; ½ teaspoon dried thyme, crushed; ½ teaspoon dried rosemary, crushed; ½ teaspoon dried savory, crushed; and ¼ teaspoon pepper. Sprinkle the mixture evenly over chicken; rub in with your fingers.

Grill chicken according to chart on page 178.

Nutrition facts per serving (using chicken pieces): 113 cal., 2 g total fat (1 g sat. fat), 50 mg chol., 312 mg sodium, 0 g carbo., 0 g fiber, 21 g pro. Daily values: 1% calcium, 7% iron

# herbed pecan rub

**Give a Southern accent to chicken or fish. The ground pecans toast and turn golden as they cook, forming a sweet, savory crust.**

**Prep: 15 minutes**
**Makes about ½ cup, enough for 3 pounds fish fillets or boneless chicken (12 servings).**

In a blender container or food processor bowl combine ½ cup broken pecans; ½ cup fresh oregano leaves; ½ cup fresh thyme leaves; 3 cloves garlic, cut up; ½ teaspoon pepper; ½ teaspoon finely shredded lemon peel; and ¼ teaspoon salt. Cover; blend or process with several on-off turns until a paste forms, stopping several times and scraping the sides.

With the machine running, gradually add ¼ cup cooking oil until mixture forms a paste. Rub onto fish or chicken. Grill fish or chicken, using indirect heat, according to charts on pages 178–180.

Nutrition facts per serving (using fish fillets): 175 cal., 9 g total fat (1 g sat. fat), 60 mg chol., 137 mg sodium, 1 g carbo., 0 g fiber, 22 g pro. Daily values: 1% vit. A, 2% calcium, 2% iron

## apple butter barbecue sauce

**Apple butter—an old-fashioned favorite for spreading on bread—is the base for this very simple sauce. Try it with chicken or pork.**

**Prep: 8 minutes**
**Makes about 1⅓ cups, enough for 1 to 2 pounds boneless poultry or pork (4 to 8 servings).**

In a small saucepan combine one 8-ounce can tomato sauce, ½ cup apple butter, and 1 tablespoon Pickapeppa sauce or Worcestershire sauce. Bring just to boiling; remove from heat.

Grill poultry or pork according to charts on pages 178–179, brushing occasionally with sauce the last 10 minutes of grilling. Heat any remaining sauce just until bubbly, stirring occasionally. Serve sauce with poultry or pork.

Nutrition facts per serving (using skinless, boneless chicken): 215 cal., 4 g total fat (1 g sat. fat), 59 mg chol., 432 mg sodium, 22 g carbo., 1 g fiber, 22 g pro. Daily values: 6% vit. A, 15% vit. C, 2% calcium, 10% iron

## honey-peach sauce

**This sweet sauce is the taste of summer boiled down to the basics: juicy peaches, honey, zingy cracked black pepper, and fresh thyme.**

**Prep: 25 minutes**
**Makes about 1¾ cups, enough for 2 to 3 pounds boneless pork or beef (8 to 12 servings).**

Peel and cut up 3 medium peaches. Place in a blender container. Add 2 tablespoons lemon juice, 2 tablespoons honey, and ½ teaspoon cracked pepper. Cover and blend until smooth. Transfer to a saucepan. Bring to boiling; reduce heat. Simmer, uncovered, about 15 minutes or until slightly thickened, stirring occasionally. Peel and finely chop 1 medium peach; stir into the sauce. Stir in 1 to 2 teaspoons snipped fresh thyme.

Grill meat according to chart on page 179, brushing with sauce the last 15 minutes of grilling. Heat remaining sauce until bubbly. Serve with meat.

Nutrition facts per serving (using boneless pork loin chops): 189 cal., 7 g total fat (3 g sat. fat), 51 mg chol., 39 mg sodium, 14 g carbo., 1 g fiber, 17 g pro. Daily values: 40% vit. A,12% vit. C, 5% iron

## five-alarm sauce

**If you can't get to Kansas City, Houston, or some other smoke-and-fire hub, turn your backyard into BBQ central with this multispiced sauce.**

**Prep: 15 minutes Cook: 5 minutes**
**Makes 2½ cups, enough for 2 to 3 pounds boneless beef or poultry (12 servings).**

In a small saucepan stir together 1 cup catsup; 1 large tomato, peeled, seeded, and chopped; 1 small green pepper, chopped; 2 tablespoons chopped onion; 2 tablespoons brown sugar; 1 to 2 tablespoons steak sauce; 1 to 2 tablespoons Worcestershire sauce; ½ teaspoon garlic powder; ¼ teaspoon each ground nutmeg, ground cinnamon, and ground cloves; and ⅛ teaspoon each ground ginger and pepper. Bring to boiling; reduce heat. Cover; simmer about 5 minutes or until green pepper is crisp-tender. Grill beef or poultry according to charts on pages 178–179. Serve sauce with beef or chicken.

Nutrition facts per serving (using beef brisket): 173 cal., 7 g total fat (3 g sat. fat), 52 mg chol., 347 mg sodium, 10 g carbo., 1 g fiber, 17 g pro. Daily values: 3% vit. A, 19% vit. C, 1% calcium, 12% iron

## peanut saté sauce

**When the mood strikes for something slightly exotic, stir up this rich saté sauce with Thai overtones. It's particularly fitting with chicken.**

**Prep: 10 minutes**
**Makes about ½ cup sauce, enough for 2 pounds boneless meat (8 servings).**

In a small bowl stir together ¼ cup creamy peanut butter, 2 tablespoons rice vinegar or white vinegar, 2 tablespoons soy sauce, 1 teaspoon minced garlic, ½ teaspoon toasted sesame oil, and ⅛ teaspoon crushed red pepper. Stir in 2 tablespoons thinly sliced green onion.

Grill meat according to charts on pages 178–179, brushing occasionally with sauce the last 5 minutes of grilling. Heat any remaining sauce until bubbly, stirring occasionally. Serve with meat.

Nutrition facts per serving (using pork top loin chops): 235 cal., 16 g total fat (4 g sat. fat), 51 mg chol., 373 mg sodium, 4 g carbo., 1 g fiber, 20 g pro. Daily values: 1% vit. C, 6% iron

# garlic-basil marinade



**If you choose the fresh herb option, grill the meat or poultry indirectly (see tip box, page 44). Otherwise, the herbs will burn.**

**Prep: 10 minutes**
**Makes about 1 cup, enough for 2 to 2½ pounds bone-in chicken (6 servings).**

Rinse chicken; pat dry. Place chicken in a plastic bag set in a shallow dish. For marinade, combine ⅔ cup dry white wine or white wine vinegar; ⅓ cup olive oil or cooking oil; 1 thinly sliced green onion; 2 tablespoons snipped fresh basil or 2 teaspoons dried basil, crushed; 1 teaspoon sugar; and 1 teaspoon minced garlic. Pour over chicken; close bag. Marinate in refrigerator for 6 to 24 hours, turning bag occasionally. Drain chicken, reserving marinade. Grill chicken according to chart on page 178, brushing with marinade up to the last 5 minutes of grilling. Discard any remaining marinade.

Nutrition facts per serving (using meaty chicken pieces): 235 cal., 14 g total fat (3 g sat. fat), 69 mg chol., 62 mg sodium, 1 g carbo., 0 g fiber, 22 g pro. Daily values: 2% vit. A, 1% calcium, 6% iron

# herb-dijon marinade

**Robust mustard and the distinctive flavor of lamb make ideal partners. The combination of herbs adds a pleasant taste twist. Also try it on beef.**

**Prep: 10 minutes**
**Makes about 1⅓ cups, enough for 5 to 6 pounds bone-in lamb or beef (12 to 14 servings).**

Place meat in a shallow dish. Combine one 8-ounce jar (¾ cup) Dijon-style mustard; ⅓ cup dry white wine; ¼ cup cooking oil; 1 teaspoon dried rosemary, crushed; 1 teaspoon dried basil, crushed; 1 teaspoon minced garlic; ½ teaspoon dried oregano, crushed; ½ teaspoon dried thyme, crushed; and ¼ teaspoon pepper. Spread over meat. Cover; marinate at room temperature 1 hour or in refrigerator 2 to 24 hours.

Drain meat, reserving marinade. Cover; refrigerate marinade until ready to serve. Grill meat according to chart on page 179. Heat marinade until bubbly, stirring occasionally. Serve with meat.

Nutrition facts per serving (using leg of lamb): 240 cal., 13 g total fat (3 g sat. fat), 77 mg chol., 536 mg sodium, 2 g carbo., 0 g fiber, 25 g pro. Daily values: 1% calcium, 13% iron

## ginger-rum marinade

**Get a taste of the tropics in every bite of beef, pork, or chicken with this terrific island-inspired, pineapple-flavored marinade.**

---

**Prep: 5 minutes**
**Makes about 1¼ cups, enough for 2 pounds boneless meat (8 servings).**

Place meat in a plastic bag set in a shallow dish. For marinade, combine ½ cup unsweetened pineapple juice, ⅓ cup rum, ¼ cup soy sauce, 1 tablespoon brown sugar, 1 tablespoon grated gingerroot, 1 teaspoon bottled minced garlic, and ¼ teaspoon ground red pepper. Pour over meat; close bag. Marinate in refrigerator for 4 to 8 hours, turning the bag occasionally.

Drain meat, reserving marinade. Grill the meat according to the charts on pages 178–179, brushing occasionally with marinade up to the last 5 minutes. Discard any remaining marinade.

Nutrition facts per serving (using boneless beef sirloin steaks): 215 cal., 10 g total fat (4 g sat. fat), 76 mg chol., 228 mg sodium, 2 g carbo., 0 g fiber, 26 g pro. Daily values: 1% vit. C, 19% iron

## lemon-rosemary marinade

**Rosemary, an herb with an assertive flavor, adds interest to this refreshing lemon marinade for fish, seafood, or chicken.**

---

**Prep: 8 minutes**
**Makes about ¾ cup, enough for 1 to 1½ pounds fish fillets or boneless poultry (4 to 6 servings).**

Rinse fish; pat dry. Place in a plastic bag set in a shallow dish. Combine 1 teaspoon finely shredded lemon peel; ⅓ cup lemon juice; ¼ cup olive oil or cooking oil; ¼ cup white wine Worcestershire sauce; 1 tablespoon sugar; 1 tablespoon snipped fresh rosemary or 1 teaspoon dried rosemary, crushed; ¼ teaspoon salt; and ⅛ teaspoon pepper. Pour over fish; close bag. Marinate in refrigerator for 1 to 2 hours, turning bag occasionally. Drain, reserving marinade. Grill fish according to charts on pages 178–179, brushing with marinade up to the last 5 minutes. Discard any remaining marinade.

Nutrition facts per serving (using fish fillets): 151 cal., 6 g total fat (1 g sat. fat), 60 mg chol., 179 mg sodium, 3 g carbo., 0 g fiber, 21 g pro. Daily values: 1% vit. A, 6% vit. C, 1% calcium, 2% iron

# get outdoors & get grilling!

**Grilling out just got more exciting. These days, a meal cooked over the coals means more than just meat. *Great Grilling & Casual Cookouts* features dinners loaded with fresh and flavorful produce, seasonings, and herbs. The results will send your family dashing to your outdoor dining room as soon as they catch the aromas wafting from the grill. Take advantage of menus that can be cooked entirely on the grill, and serve up wholesome foods that are anything but predictable. *Great Grilling & Casual Cookouts* helps you move the weeknight kitchen or the Saturday night party outdoors so you can savor great food, good company, and fresh air.**

# fire up for beef, pork, and lamb

# grilled beef, red onion, & blue cheese salad

**The natural sweetness of red onions is intensified when the onions are brushed with a balsamic vinaigrette and grilled alongside sirloin steak. Aromatic grilled herb bread makes a perfect go-along to this crisp and hearty main-dish salad.**



**Prep: 15 minutes Grill: 8 minutes Makes 4 servings**

- **2 tablespoons olive oil**
- **3 tablespoons balsamic vinegar**
- **1 clove garlic, minced**
- **1 boneless beef sirloin steak, cut 1 inch thick (about ¾ pound)**
- **1 tablespoon snipped fresh thyme**
- **2 teaspoons snipped fresh rosemary**
- **4 ¼-inch-thick slices red onion**
- **6 cups lightly packed mesclun or torn mixed salad greens**
- **2 tablespoons crumbled Gorgonzola or blue cheese**
- **8 yellow and/or red pear tomatoes, halved**

For vinaigrette, in a screw-top jar combine oil, vinegar, garlic, ½ teaspoon salt, and ½ teaspoon pepper; cover and shake well. Trim fat from steak. Remove 1 tablespoon vinaigrette from jar and brush evenly onto both sides of steak. Press thyme and rosemary onto both sides of the steak. Brush both sides of onion slices with some of the remaining vinaigrette, reserving the rest; set aside.

Grill steak on rack of an uncovered grill directly over medium heat to desired doneness, turning once. (Allow 8 to 12 minutes for medium-rare and 12 to 15 minutes for medium doneness.) For last 10 minutes of grilling, place onions on grill rack beside meat. Grill onions until tender, turning once.

Divide mesclun among 4 dinner plates. To serve, thinly slice the steak across the grain. Separate onion slices into rings. Arrange warm steak and onions atop mesclun. Drizzle with the reserved vinaigrette. Top with cheese and tomatoes.

Nutrition facts per serving: 266 cal., 16 g total fat (5 g sat. fat), 59 mg chol., 373 mg sodium, 9 g carbo., 2 g fiber, 22 g pro. Daily values: 7% vit. A, 28% vit. C, 4% calcium, 22% iron

### Serving suggestion:

*While you're enjoying this salad, put Nectarine-Raspberry Crisp (page 171) on the grill for dessert.*

# steak rémoulade sandwiches

**Served in France as an accompaniment to cold meats, fish, and seafood, the classic mayonnaise-based sauce called rémoulade adds a hint of rustic sophistication to this steak sandwich perked up by peppery arugula and grilled sweet peppers.**



- ¼ cup light mayonnaise dressing or salad dressing
- 1½ teaspoons finely minced cornichons or gherkins
- 1 teaspoon capers, chopped
- ¼ teaspoon lemon juice
- 2 8-ounce boneless beef loin strip steaks
- 2 teaspoons prepared garlic spread or 2 teaspoons bottled minced garlic
- 1 large yellow sweet pepper, seeded and cut lengthwise into 8 strips
- 4 kaiser or French-style rolls, split
- 1 cup arugula or spinach leaves

**Serving suggestion:**

*Accompany this hearty sandwich with crisp purchased coleslaw and baked potato chips.*

**Prep: 15 minutes Grill: 8 minutes Makes 4 servings**

For rémoulade, in a small bowl combine mayonnaise dressing, cornichons, capers, lemon juice, and a pinch freshly ground black pepper. Cover and refrigerate until needed.

Pat steaks dry with a paper towel. Rub garlic spread over steaks. Sprinkle with additional freshly ground black pepper. Grill steaks and sweet pepper strips on rack of an uncovered grill directly over medium heat until meat is desired doneness, turning once. (Allow 8 to 12 minutes for medium-rare and 12 to 15 minutes for medium doneness.) Transfer cooked steaks and sweet pepper strips to a cutting board; cut steaks into ¼-inch-thick slices.

If desired, grill rolls directly over medium heat about 1 minute or until toasted. Spread rémoulade on bottom halves of rolls; top with arugula, steak slices, sweet pepper, and roll tops.

Nutrition facts per serving: 380 cal., 13 g total fat (3 g sat. fat), 65 mg chol., 516 mg sodium, 37 g carbo., 0 g fiber, 29 g pro. Daily values: 2% vit. A, 144% vit. C, 6% calcium, 29% iron

# jerk london broil

**Got a hankering for a little heat? The small Scotch bonnet pepper—one of the hottest peppers on the planet and a star in Jamaican cooking—packs a powerful punch. If you can't find a Scotch bonnet or want less heat, substitute a jalapeño pepper.**



**Prep:** 10 minutes **Marinate:** Up to 24 hours
**Grill:** 12 minutes **Makes** 6 servings

- 4 green onions
- 1 1-inch piece fresh ginger, sliced
- 1 Scotch bonnet pepper, stem and seeds removed (optional)
- 2 tablespoons cooking oil
- 3 cloves garlic
- 2 teaspoons Jamaican jerk seasoning
- ¼ cup lime juice
- 1 1¼- to 1½-pound beef flank steak

For jerk marinade, combine all ingredients except steak in a blender container; cover and blend until smooth. Diagonally score both sides of the steak at 1-inch intervals, making a diamond pattern. Place the steak in a glass dish; spread the marinade over the steak. Grill right away or cover steak with plastic wrap and marinate in the refrigerator for up to 24 hours.

Grill the steak on the rack of an uncovered grill directly over medium heat to desired doneness, turning once. (Allow 12 to 14 minutes for medium doneness.) Transfer the steak to a cutting board; cut across the grain into ⅛- to ¼-inch-thick slices.

Nutrition facts per serving: 187 cal., 11 g total fat (3 g sat. fat), 44 mg chol., 117 mg sodium, 2 g carbo., 0 g fiber, 18 g pro. Daily values: 4% vit. A, 8% vit. C, 1% calcium, 13% iron

### Serving suggestion:

*Top off this island-style steak with a side of Sweet & Spicy Pepper-Pineapple Salsa* (*page 163*).

### this **jerk** is all **wet**

Jerk seasoning—a powerful and pungent spice mixture of chile peppers, thyme, cinnamon, ginger, allspice, and cloves—is most often used as a dry rub for meats. But jerk can be "wet," too. That simply means the jerk spices—along with onions and/or garlic—are mixed with some kind of liquid to make a marinade.

# sun-dried **tomato** burgers

**Burgers on the grill take on a whole new meaning when they're infused with fresh lemon, studded with dried tomatoes, and slathered with a basil mayonnaise dressing zipped up with a jalapeño pepper.**



**Prep: 15 minutes Grill: 14 minutes Makes 4 servings**

- **1 pound lean ground beef**
- **1 tablespoon finely chopped, drained, oil-packed sun-dried tomatoes**
- **1 teaspoon finely shredded lemon or lime peel**
- **¼ cup light mayonnaise dressing or salad dressing**
- **2 tablespoons snipped fresh basil**
- **1 jalapeño pepper, seeded and finely chopped**
- **4 onion hamburger buns**
- **1 cup lightly packed arugula or spinach leaves**

In a medium bowl combine beef, tomatoes, lemon peel, ½ teaspoon salt, and ¼ teaspoon pepper; mix lightly but thoroughly. Shape into four ½-inch-thick patties. Grill patties on the rack of an uncovered grill directly over medium heat for 14 to 18 minutes or until no pink remains, turning once.

Meanwhile, in a small bowl combine mayonnaise dressing, basil, and jalapeño pepper; mix well. For the last 1 to 2 minutes of grilling, place buns, cut sides down, on grill rack to toast. Top bottom halves of buns with burgers. Top with mayonnaise dressing mixture and arugula. Add bun tops.

Nutrition facts per serving: 450 cal., 20 g total fat (6 g sat. fat), 71 mg chol., 784 mg sodium, 40 g carbo., 2 g fiber, 26 g pro. Daily values: 1% vit. A, 13% vit. C, 6% calcium, 25% iron

**Serving suggestion:**

*Grilled Eggplant Salad (page 167) or Grilled Antipasto Skewers (page 157) makes a perfect side for these Italian-style burgers.*

# herbed tenderloin steaks & vegetables

**A bouquet of herbs, beautiful tomatoes, and asparagus lends fresh-from-the-garden flavor to this meat-and-vegetables meal. Stir purchased roasted garlic into deli mashed potatoes and serve up French bread to complete a patio-perfect repast.**



- **2 cloves garlic**
- **¼ cup loosely packed fresh basil leaves**
- **2 tablespoons fresh thyme leaves**
- **1 tablespoon fresh rosemary**
- **1 tablespoon fresh mint leaves**
- **2 tablespoons olive oil**
- **½ teaspoon salt**
- **½ teaspoon pepper**
- **4 beef tenderloin steaks, cut 1 inch thick (about 1 pound)**
- **2 large yellow tomatoes, halved crosswise**
- **1 pound asparagus spears, trimmed**

**Serving suggestion:**

*For dessert, try Bananas Suzette over Grilled Pound Cake (page 175).*

**Prep: 15 minutes Grill: 8 minutes Makes 4 servings**

With food processor or blender running, add garlic through feed tube or lid. Process or blend until garlic is finely chopped. Add basil, thyme, rosemary, and mint. Cover and process or blend until herbs are chopped. With food processor or blender running, add oil in a thin, steady stream. (When necessary, stop food processor or blender and use a rubber scraper to scrape the sides of bowl or container.) Stir in salt and pepper.

Spread some of the herb mixture evenly over both sides of the steaks and over cut sides of tomatoes; set aside. Fold 18×12-inch piece of heavy foil in half to make a double thickness of foil that measures 9×12 inches. Place asparagus in the center of the foil. Add remaining herb mixture, turning asparagus to coat evenly. Grill steaks and asparagus (on foil) on the rack of an uncovered grill directly over medium heat for 5 minutes. Turn steaks and asparagus spears; add tomatoes to grill. Grill until steaks are desired doneness. (Allow 3 to 7 minutes more for medium-rare and 7 to 10 minutes more for medium doneness.) Grill vegetables until asparagus is crisp-tender and tomatoes are hot (do not turn).

Nutrition facts per serving: 245 cal., 14 g total fat (4 g sat. fat), 65 mg chol., 322 mg sodium, 6 g carbo., 2 g fiber, 24 g pro. Daily values: 8% vit. A, 47% vit. C, 3% calcium, 3% iron

# flank steak on tap

**Hearty pub food like this beer-marinated beef steak is back in style for good reason—it's warm and welcoming. On a cool fall evening, enjoy it outdoors with the seasonal colors, an Oktoberfest brew, and, of course, lots of good conversation.**



Prep: 20 minutes Marinate: 4 to 24 hours
Grill: 12 minutes Makes 4 servings

- 1 large onion, thinly sliced
- ¾ cup beer
- 3 tablespoons Worcestershire sauce
- 2 tablespoons brown sugar
- 3 cloves garlic, minced
- 1 bay leaf
- ¼ teaspoon coarsely ground pepper
- 1 1¼- to 1½-pound beef flank steak
- ¼ teaspoon salt
- 2 teaspoons cornstarch
- Snipped fresh parsley (optional)
- Coarsely ground pepper (optional)

For marinade, in a small saucepan combine onion, beer, Worcestershire sauce, brown sugar, garlic, bay leaf, and the ¼ teaspoon pepper. Bring to boiling; reduce heat. Simmer, uncovered, for 4 to 5 minutes or until sugar is dissolved and onion and garlic are beginning to soften. Cool to room temperature. Diagonally score both sides of the steak at 1-inch intervals, making a diamond pattern. Place the steak in a plastic bag set in a shallow dish. Pour marinade over steak; close bag. Marinate in refrigerator for at least 4 hours or up to 24 hours, turning occasionally.

Drain steak, reserving marinade. Remove bay leaf. Season steak with salt. Grill on rack of an uncovered grill directly over medium heat to desired doneness, turning once. (Allow 12 to 14 minutes for medium doneness.) Meanwhile, for sauce, in a small saucepan combine reserved marinade and cornstarch. Cook and stir over medium heat until the sauce is thickened and bubbly. Cook and stir 2 minutes more. To serve, cut steak across the grain into ⅛- to ¼-inch-thick slices; spoon sauce over steak. If desired, sprinkle with parsley and additional pepper.

Nutrition facts per serving: 185 cal., 7 g total fat (3 g sat. fat), 44 mg chol., 221 mg sodium, 10 g carbo., 1 g fiber, 17 g pro. Daily values: 0% vit. A, 25% vit. C, 2% calcium, 16% iron

**Serving suggestion:**

*Add steamed green beans and mashed potatoes and dinner's done!*

# veal chops with pesto-stuffed mushrooms

**Short on time tonight? Briefly soak tender veal chops in a white wine-sage marinade and toss them on the grill. Short on time tomorrow? Marinate the meat overnight for a dinner in no time and for more flavorful chops, too (pictured on cover).**



- **4 veal loin chops, cut ¾ inch thick (about 1¼ pounds)**
- **¼ cup dry white wine**
- **3 large cloves garlic, minced**
- **1 tablespoon snipped fresh sage or thyme**
- **1 tablespoon white wine Worcestershire sauce**
- **1 tablespoon olive oil**
- **8 large fresh mushrooms (2 to 2½ inches in diameter)**
- **2 to 3 tablespoons prepared pesto**

**Serving suggestion:**

*Slender steamed baby carrots and hot cooked rice round out this meal.*

**Prep: 10 minutes Marinate: 15 minutes to 24 hours**
**Grill: 12 minutes Makes 4 servings**

For marinade, combine wine, garlic, herb, Worcestershire sauce, and oil. Place veal chops in a large plastic bag set in a shallow dish. Pour over chops; close bag. Marinate at room temperature for 15 minutes. (Or, marinate in refrigerator for up to 24 hours, turning bag occasionally.)

Drain veal chops, reserving marinade. Sprinkle chops with freshly ground black pepper. Grill chops on the rack of an uncovered grill directly over medium heat to desired doneness, turning and brushing with marinade halfway through cooking. (Allow 12 to 14 minutes for medium-rare and 15 to 17 minutes for medium doneness.)

Meanwhile, carefully remove stems from mushrooms; chop stems for another use or discard. Brush mushroom caps with reserved marinade; place mushrooms, stem sides down, on grill rack. Grill for 4 minutes. Turn stem sides up; spoon some pesto into each. Grill about 4 minutes more or until heated through. Serve mushrooms with veal chops.

Nutrition facts per serving: 285 cal., 16 g total fat (2 g sat. fat), 100 mg chol., 157 mg sodium, 4 g carbo., 1 g fiber, 28 g pro. Daily values: 0% vit. A, 3% vit. C, 3% calcium, 9% iron

# mesquite mixed grill

**Can't decide between pork chops and sausage? Have both! The sweet smoke of mesquite infuses this mixed grill with an unmistakably good flavor. A sauce made with mustard (try any whole-grain variety that suits you) makes a stylish condiment.**



- 2 cups mesquite wood chips
- 4 boneless pork top loin chops, cut ¾ inch thick (about 1 pound)
- 4 small leeks or 1 medium red sweet pepper, seeded and cut into 1-inch pieces
- ⅛ teaspoon garlic salt
- ¼ teaspoon black pepper
- 8 ounces fully cooked turkey Polish sausage, cut into 4 equal portions
- ⅓ cup whole-grain mustard
- 2 teaspoons white wine vinegar or cider vinegar
- 1 teaspoon snipped fresh tarragon

**Serving suggestion:**

*Serve this hearty meat mixture with grilled garlic bread.*

**Prep:** 10 minutes **Grill:** 9 minutes **Makes** 4 servings

At least 1 hour before grilling, soak wood chips in enough water to cover. Trim fat from pork chops. If using leeks, rinse well, trim root end, and cut 3 to 4 inches off each top and discard. Sprinkle garlic salt and black pepper evenly over chops and leeks or sweet pepper.

Drain wood chips. In a grill with a cover arrange preheated coals in even layer. Sprinkle wood chips onto coals. Place the chops and leeks or sweet pepper on grill rack directly over medium coals; cover grill and cook for 5 minutes. Turn chops; add the sausage to grill. Cover and grill 4 to 6 minutes more or until the chops are slightly pink in center and juices run clear, turning sausage once.

Meanwhile, combine mustard, vinegar, and tarragon. Serve as a dipping sauce with chops, sausages, and leeks or sweet pepper.

Nutrition facts per serving: 282 cal., 12 g total fat (3 g sat. fat), 86 mg chol., 880 mg sodium, 12 g carbo., 4 g fiber, 27 g pro. Daily values: 0% vit. A, 29% vit. C, 7% calcium, 19% iron

## smoke 'em

Tossing wood chips on your grill gives foods a wood-smoked aroma and flavor. Generally, wood chips need to be soaked in enough water to cover them for about an hour. Afterwards drain the wood chips well and toss onto hot coals. Good choices for wood chips include mesquite, alder, hickory, oak, and sweetish fruitwoods such as apple, cherry, and peach.

# pork chops with savory mushroom stuffing

**There's a surprise inside the pocket of these quick-cooking boneless pork chops—a mouthwatering mushroom stuffing. Instead of white button mushrooms, try using brown crimini mushrooms for even more mushroom flavor.**



**Prep: 15 minutes Grill: 20 minutes Makes 4 servings**

- 2 teaspoons olive oil
- 2 tablespoons thinly sliced green onions
- 1 8-ounce package fresh mushrooms, coarsely chopped
- 2 teaspoons snipped fresh rosemary or oregano
- ⅛ teaspoon salt
- ⅛ teaspoon pepper
- 4 boneless pork loin chops, cut 1 inch thick
- 2 teaspoons Worcestershire sauce

For stuffing, in a large skillet heat oil over medium heat. Add green onion and cook for 1 minute. Stir in mushrooms, rosemary, salt, and pepper. Cook and stir 2 to 3 minutes more or until mushrooms are tender. Remove from heat.

Trim fat from chops. Make a pocket in each chop by cutting from fat side almost to, but not through, the opposite side. Spoon stuffing into pockets in chops. If necessary, secure with wooden toothpicks.

Brush chops with Worcestershire sauce. Season chops lightly with additional salt and pepper. Grill chops on the rack of an uncovered grill directly over medium heat about 20 minutes or until juices run clear, turning once. To serve, remove wooden toothpicks.

Nutrition facts per serving: 241 cal., 14 g total fat (4 g sat. fat), 77 mg chol., 218 mg sodium, 4 g carbo., 1 g fiber, 25 g pro. Daily values: 1% vit. A, 13% vit. C, 1% calcium, 14% iron

**Serving suggestion:**

*Pair these pork chops with Warm Asparagus, Fennel, & Spinach Salad (page 161).*

# grilled italian sausage with sweet & sour peppers

**Sicilians love sweet and sour flavors and toss super-sweet raisins into their delicious meat and fish dishes with culinary abandon. Here, grilled Italian sausage is presented on a bed of piquant, sweet grilled vegetables.**



**Prep: 20 minutes Grill: 10 minutes Makes 6 servings**

- 3 tablespoons slivered almonds
- ¼ cup raisins
- 3 tablespoons red wine vinegar
- 2 tablespoons sugar
- ¼ teaspoon salt
- ⅛ teaspoon black pepper
- 1 tablespoon olive oil
- 2 green sweet peppers, cut into 1-inch-wide strips
- 2 red sweet peppers, cut into 1-inch-wide strips
- 1 medium red onion, thickly sliced
- 6 sweet Italian sausage links

In a small nonstick skillet cook and stir almonds for 1 to 2 minutes or until golden brown. Stir in raisins. Remove skillet from heat. Let stand for 1 minute. Carefully stir in vinegar, sugar, salt, and pepper. Return to heat; cook and stir just until the sugar dissolves.

Drizzle oil over sweet pepper strips and onion slices. Prick sausages several times with a fork. Grill vegetables and sausages on the rack of an uncovered grill directly over medium heat for 10 to 15 minutes or until no pink remains in the sausages and vegetables are tender, turning once.

In the large bowl toss the vegetables with the almond mixture; spoon onto a serving platter. Place sausages atop.

Nutrition facts per serving: 276 cal., 19 g total fat (6 g sat. fat), 59 mg chol., 604 mg sodium, 15 g carbo., 1 g fiber, 13 g pro. Daily values: 19% vit. A, 102% vit. C, 2% calcium, 9% iron

**Serving suggestion:**

*For more Italian goodness, grill purchased polenta alongside the sausages and vegetables.*

# grilled **mustard**-glazed pork

**This express-lane dinner gives you time to slow down as soon as you walk in the door. Simply mix up the marinade and pour it over the pork. Let it sit in the refrigerator while you unwind. Grill about 20 minutes and dinner's done!**



- **2 12- to 14-ounce pork tenderloins**
- **½ cup apple juice**
- **¼ cup cider vinegar**
- **2 large shallots, minced**
- **¼ cup coarse-grain brown mustard**
- **2 tablespoons olive oil**
- **1 tablespoon brown sugar**
- **1½ teaspoons soy sauce**
- **Dash pepper**
- **Snipped fresh chives (optional)**

### Serving suggestion:

*Try serving these sweet and savory pork tenderloins with Apple & Grilled Chicken Salad (page 126), minus the chicken.*

**Prep: 10 minutes Marinate: 30 minutes**
**Grill: 23 minutes Makes 6 servings**

Trim fat from tenderloins. Place tenderloins in a plastic bag set in a shallow dish. For marinade, combine apple juice, vinegar, shallots, mustard, oil, brown sugar, soy sauce, and pepper. Pour over meat; close bag. Marinate in refrigerator for 30 minutes, turning bag occasionally.

In a grill with a cover arrange preheated coals around a drip pan. Drain tenderloins, reserving marinade. Place tenderloins on the grill rack directly over medium-hot coals; grill for 8 minutes, turning once to brown both sides. Move tenderloins over drip pan; insert meat thermometer in center of thickest tenderloin. Cover and grill for 15 to 20 minutes more or until meat thermometer registers 160°.

Meanwhile, for sauce, pour reserved marinade into a medium saucepan. Bring to boiling and reduce heat. Simmer, uncovered, about 8 minutes or until reduced to ⅔ cup. Slice the tenderloins across the grain. Serve with the sauce. If desired, sprinkle with chives.

Nutrition facts per serving: 215 cal., 9 g total fat (2 g sat. fat), 81 mg chol., 280 mg sodium, 7 g carbo., 0 g fiber, 26 g pro. Daily values: 8% vit. A, 1% vit. C, 2% calcium, 12% iron

# fennel & pork sausage with grape relish

**Two kinds of fennel give great flavor to these spirited sausage patties. Aromatic fennel seed lends the patties its essence, and alongside the patties, crisp fresh fennel cooks with balsamic vinegar and red grapes to make an elegant sauce.**



**Prep: 15 minutes Grill: 14 minutes Makes 4 servings**

- 1 slightly beaten egg
- 1 tablespoon bourbon (optional)
- ½ cup quick-cooking rolled oats
- 1 tablespoon fennel seed, crushed
- 1 large clove garlic, minced
- 1 teaspoon finely shredded lemon peel
- 1 teaspoon paprika
- 1 pound lean ground pork
- 1½ cups red seedless grapes, halved
- 1 small fennel bulb, coarsely chopped (1 cup)
- 1 tablespoon margarine or butter
- 2 tablespoons balsamic vinegar
- ¼ cup snipped fresh parsley

In a large bowl combine the egg and, if desired, bourbon. Stir in rolled oats, fennel seed, garlic, lemon peel, paprika, ½ teaspoon salt, and ½ teaspoon pepper. Add ground pork. Mix well. Shape the pork mixture into four ¾-inch-thick patties. Set aside.

Fold a 36×18-inch piece of heavy foil in half to make a double thickness of foil that measures 18×18 inches. Place the grapes, chopped fennel, margarine, and vinegar in the center of the foil. Sprinkle with additional salt and pepper. Bring up 2 opposite edges of foil and seal with a double fold. Fold remaining edges to completely enclose the grape mixture, leaving space for steam to build.

Grill the pork patties and the grape mixture on the rack of an uncovered grill directly over medium heat for 14 to 16 minutes or until no pink remains in the patties, turning once. To serve, spoon grape mixture over the grilled patties. Sprinkle with the fresh parsley.

Nutrition facts per serving: 284 cal., 14 g total fat (5 g sat. fat), 106 mg chol., 409 mg sodium, 23 g carbo., 7 g fiber, 18 g pro. Daily values: 11% vit. A, 28% vit. C, 5% calcium, 17% iron

**Serving suggestion:**

*Hot buttered orzo is a simple side for these homemade sausage patties with grape sauce.*

# jamaican pork kabobs

**Jamaican doesn't always mean jerk. These pork and vegetable kabobs get an island air from mango chutney and a liberal dose of Pickapeppa sauce, a much milder version of its famous relative, Tabasco. Cool the fire with slices of mango and lime.**



- **2 ears of corn, husked and cleaned**
- **1 12- to 14-ounce pork tenderloin**
- **1 small red onion, cut into ½-inch-thick wedges**
- **16 baby pattypan squash, about 1 inch in diameter, or 4 tomatillos, quartered**
- **¼ cup mango chutney, finely chopped**
- **3 tablespoons Pickapeppa sauce**
- **1 tablespoon cooking oil**
- **1 tablespoon water**

**Serving suggestion:**

*Present these kabobs on a bed of hot cooked rice, and follow up with Grilled Fruit Kabobs with Lime-Yogurt Sauce (page 172).*

**Prep: 15 minutes Grill: 12 minutes Makes 4 servings**

Cut corn crosswise into 1-inch pieces. In medium saucepan cook corn pieces in small amount of boiling water for 3 minutes; drain and rinse with cold water. Meanwhile, cut tenderloin into 1-inch-thick slices. For kabobs, on long metal skewers alternately thread tenderloin, onion, squash or tomatillos, and corn.

In small bowl combine chutney, Pickapeppa sauce, oil, and water; set aside. Grill kabobs on the rack of an uncovered grill directly over medium heat for 12 to 14 minutes or until no pink remains in the pork and the vegetables are tender, turning once and brushing with the chutney mixture during the last 5 minutes of grilling.

Nutrition facts per serving: 252 cal., 7 g total fat (2 g sat. fat), 60 mg chol., 127 mg sodium, 27 g carbo., 3 g fiber, 21 g pro. Daily values: 3% vit. A, 13% vit. C, 2% calcium, 10% iron

## summer supper **sippers**

Warm summer evenings call for cooling drinks. Consider these:

- Sparkling water with fruit-juice cubes (orange, cranberry, mango, or papaya juice frozen in ice cube trays) and fresh mint.
- Spritzers made with sparkling water, cranberry juice, and a lime twist.
- Special iced teas, made with brewed green, herbal, or raspberry- or currant-flavored black tea.

# grilled lamb chops with mint marinade

**Petite lamb chops are pretty on their own—what's even more attractive about these chops is that they can marinate in the refrigerator overnight and are ready to eat after about 10 minutes of grilling. Serve them with wedges of fresh lemon.**



- **8 well-trimmed lamb loin chops, cut 1 inch thick (about 2 pounds)**
- **2 tablespoons lemon juice**
- **2 tablespoons olive oil**
- **3 cloves garlic, minced**
- **¼ cup snipped fresh mint**
- **¼ teaspoon pepper**
- **¼ teaspoon salt**

### Serving suggestion:

*Jasmine-Mint Tea Rice with Peas (page 159) is the perfect foil for these tender chops.*

**Prep: 10 minutes Marinate: 30 minutes to 24 hours**
**Grill: 10 minutes Makes 4 servings**

Trim fat from chops. Place chops in a plastic bag set in a shallow dish. For marinade, combine lemon juice, oil, garlic, 3 tablespoons of the mint, and the pepper. Pour over the chops; close bag. Marinate in the refrigerator for at least 30 minutes or up to 24 hours. Drain chops, discarding marinade. Sprinkle chops with the salt.

Grill chops on rack of an uncovered grill directly over medium heat to desired doneness, turning once. (Allow 10 to 14 minutes for medium-rare and 14 to 16 minutes for medium doneness.) Sprinkle with remaining mint.

Nutrition facts per serving: 310 cal., 18 g total fat (5 g sat. fat), 107 mg chol., 229 mg sodium, 2 g carbo., 0 g fiber, 34 g pro. Daily values: 1% vit. A, 12% vit. C, 2% calcium, 21% iron

## make mine **marinated**

A good soak is good for the soul—and it's good for your food, too. Marinating is great in two ways: it adds flavor and it tenderizes meats. Generally marinades are made with an acidic liquid (which has the tenderizing effect) such as wine, vinegar, or citrus juice, plus herbs and seasonings—and sometimes a little oil. The longer the meat spends luxuriating in the liquid, the more great flavor it will have.

# grilled greek leg of lamb

**Leg of lamb in less than an hour? You bet, if it's sliced thin and flash-grilled after a quick soak in a lemon-oregano marinade. A sauce of grilled tomatoes mixed with cinnamon, feta cheese, and Greek olives adds an authentic taste of the islands.**



**Prep:** 20 minutes **Marinate:** 20 minutes to 24 hours
**Grill:** 8 minutes **Makes** 6 servings

- 1½ to 2 pounds boneless leg of lamb, trimmed
- 1 tablespoon finely shredded lemon peel
- ⅔ cup lemon juice
- 6 tablespoons olive oil
- ⅓ cup snipped fresh oregano
- ¼ cup pitted, sliced kalamata olives
- ½ cup snipped fresh parsley
- ½ cup crumbled feta cheese
- ¼ teaspoon ground cinnamon
- 2 pounds plum tomatoes

Slice lamb across grain into ½- to ¾-inch-thick pieces; place in a large bowl. For marinade, stir together the lemon peel, half of the lemon juice, 4 tablespoons of the oil, the oregano, ½ teaspoon salt, and ⅛ teaspoon pepper. Cover and marinate at room temperature for 20 minutes. (Or, place lamb in a plastic bag set in a shallow dish. Pour marinade over lamb; close bag. Marinate in the refrigerator for at least 8 hours or up to 24 hours, turning bag occasionally.) In a large bowl combine remaining lemon juice, olives, 1 tablespoon of the remaining oil, the parsley, feta cheese, cinnamon, and ¼ teaspoon pepper; set aside.

Drain lamb, discard marinade. Brush tomatoes with the remaining 1 tablespoon oil. Grill lamb and tomatoes on the rack of an uncovered grill directly over medium-hot heat for 8 to 10 minutes or until lamb is desired doneness and tomatoes are slightly charred, turning once. Transfer tomatoes to cutting board; cool slightly and slice. Toss the tomatoes with the feta cheese mixture; serve with lamb.

Nutrition facts per serving: 256 cal., 14 g total fat (4 g sat. fat), 66 mg chol., 493 mg sodium, 11 g carbo., 0 g fiber, 22 g pro. Daily values: 15% vit. A, 80% vit. C, 6% calcium, 18% iron

### Serving suggestion:

*While the lamb is grilling, cook some couscous to soak up the sauce from the fresh tomatoes.*

# tandoori-style lamb chops

**You don't need the traditional Indian brick-and-clay oven called a tandoor to make these chops, but the delicious characteristic of tandoori cuisine—quick cooking to seal in juices and flavors—is present in these Indian-spiced lamb chops.**



**Prep: 20 minutes Grill: 10 minutes Makes 4 servings**

- 2 tablespoons cooking oil
- 6 cloves garlic, minced
- 2 teaspoons grated fresh ginger
- 1 tablespoon garam masala*
- 8 well-trimmed lamb loin chops, cut 1 inch thick (about 2 pounds)
- 2 medium yellow summer squash and/or zucchini, halved lengthwise
- 4 pita bread rounds
- ½ cup plain low-fat yogurt
- 1 tablespoon snipped fresh mint
- ¼ cup chutney or hot chutney

In small bowl combine oil, garlic, ginger, garam masala, and ½ teaspoon salt. Brush onto all sides of the chops and squash.

Grill chops and squash on the rack of an uncovered grill directly over medium heat to desired doneness and until squash is tender, turning once. (Allow 10 to 14 minutes for medium-rare doneness.) For the last 2 minutes of grilling, place pita rounds on grill rack to heat.

Meanwhile, in a small bowl combine yogurt and mint. Transfer vegetables to a cutting board; cool slightly and slice diagonally ½ inch thick. Serve squash, pita bread, and chutney with chops.

Nutrition facts per serving: 615 cal., 22 g total fat (6 g sat. fat), 135 mg chol., 735 mg sodium, 51 g carbo., 1 g fiber, 51 g pro. Daily values: 3% vit. A, 11% vit. C, 14% calcium, 40% iron

**Note: For homemade garam masala, combine 1 teaspoon ground cumin, 1 teaspoon ground coriander, ½ teaspoon pepper, ½ teaspoon ground cardamom, ¼ teaspoon ground cinnamon, and ¼ teaspoon ground cloves.*

### Serving suggestion:

*Start out this meal with papdum, crisp black-pepper and lentil crackers, found at Indian markets.*

# the perfect bird

# grilled vietnamese chicken breasts

**This is no ho-hum chicken sandwich. Spicy-sweet peanut sauce and crisp broccoli slaw lend an Asian accent to this out-of-the-ordinary grilled chicken.**



**Prep: 15 minutes Grill: 12 minutes Makes 4 servings**

- 4 medium skinless, boneless chicken breast halves (about 1 pound total)
- 2 teaspoons toasted sesame oil
- ½ teaspoon crushed red pepper
- 2 tablespoons sugar
- 2 tablespoons peanut butter
- 2 tablespoons soy sauce
- 1 tablespoon cooking oil
- 1 clove garlic, minced
- 4 French-style rolls, split
- ¼ cup radish sprouts
- ½ cup packaged shredded broccoli (broccoli slaw mix)
- ¼ cup chopped peanuts (optional)

Rinse chicken; pat dry. Combine sesame oil and crushed red pepper; brush over chicken.

Grill chicken on the lightly greased rack of an uncovered grill directly over medium heat for 12 to 15 minutes or until tender and no longer pink, turning once.

Meanwhile, for sauce, in a small saucepan,* stir together sugar, peanut butter, soy sauce, oil, garlic, and 2 tablespoons water. Heat on grill rack until sugar is dissolved, stirring frequently. For the last 1 minute of grilling, place split rolls on the grill rack to toast.

To serve, place cooked chicken breasts on bottom halves of rolls; spoon on sauce and top with radish sprouts, broccoli, peanuts (if desired), and roll tops.

Nutrition facts per serving: 360 cal., 14 g total fat (3 g sat. fat), 59 mg chol., 852 mg sodium, 29 g carbo., 1 g fiber, 28 g pro. Daily values: 3% vit. A, 14% vit. C, 4% calcium, 14% iron

**Note: The heat from the grill will blacken the outside of the saucepan, so use an old one or a small cast-iron skillet.*

**Serving suggestion:**

*Serve these sandwiches with a homemade Asian-style salad of paper-thin-sliced cucumber dressed with a bottled sesame vinaigrette.*

# curried chicken & potato packets

**Unwrap a little fun tonight! You'll curry favor from your family with the Indian flavors of chicken and vegetables cooked in a velvety sour cream sauce. Individual serving packets give this dish flair—precooked chicken strips make it fast.**



- **1 9-ounce package frozen cooked chicken breast strips**
- **4 medium potatoes, cut into ¾-inch cubes**
- **1½ cups packaged peeled baby carrots**
- **1 small onion, thinly sliced**
- **½ cup dairy sour cream or plain low-fat yogurt**
- **1 teaspoon curry powder**
- **1 teaspoon Dijon-style mustard**
- **½ teaspoon salt**
- **½ teaspoon paprika**
- **⅛ teaspoon crushed red pepper**

**Serving suggestion:**

*Something spicy calls for something sweet. Try Honey-Glazed Bananas (page 162) as a side.*

**Prep: 10 minutes Grill: 25 minutes Makes 4 servings**

Tear off four 24×18-inch pieces of heavy foil. Fold each piece in half to make a double thickness of foil that measures 12×18 inches; set aside.

In a large bowl combine frozen chicken, potatoes, carrots, and onion; set aside. In a small bowl combine sour cream, curry powder, mustard, salt, paprika, and crushed red pepper. Pour over chicken mixture; toss gently.

Divide mixture among the foil pieces. Bring up opposite long edges of a foil piece and seal with a double fold. Fold ends to completely enclose chicken mixture, leaving space for steam to build. Repeat with remaining pieces of foil.

Grill the chicken mixture on the rack of an uncovered grill directly over medium heat about 25 minutes or until vegetables are tender.

Nutrition facts per serving: 371 cal., 11 g total fat (5 g sat. fat), 70 mg chol., 414 mg sodium, 44 g carbo., 3 g fiber, 24 g pro. Daily values: 129% vit. A, 41% vit. C, 6% calcium, 21% iron

# grilled asian chicken & noodles

**Keep a cool noodle with this quick-to-fix dish. Cold udon noodles flavored with sesame-ginger dressing are tossed with crisp cabbage, warm chicken, and eggplant. Look for udon—a thick Japanese noodle similar to spaghetti—at Asian markets.**



**Prep:** 20 minutes **Grill:** 12 minutes
**Cool:** 5 minutes **Makes** 4 servings

- 8 ounces udon or Chinese curly noodles
- ¼ cup light soy sauce
- 2 tablespoons toasted sesame oil
- 2 tablespoons rice vinegar
- 4 cloves garlic, minced
- 1½ teaspoons grated fresh ginger
- ¼ teaspoon crushed red pepper
- 4 medium skinless, boneless chicken breast halves (about 1 pound total)
- 1 small eggplant, sliced
- 4 cups packaged shredded cabbage with carrot (coleslaw mix)
- ¼ cup chopped cashews (optional)
- 2 to 3 tablespoons chopped fresh cilantro

Cook noodles according to package directions. Meanwhile, combine soy sauce, sesame oil, vinegar, garlic, ginger, and crushed red pepper. Set 2 tablespoons of the soy sauce mixture aside. Drain noodles. In a large bowl toss noodles with the remaining soy sauce mixture. Place noodle mixture in freezer to quick chill.

Rinse chicken; pat dry. Grill chicken on the lightly greased rack of an uncovered grill directly over medium heat for 12 to 15 minutes or until chicken is tender and no longer pink, turning once and brushing occasionally with the reserved soy sauce mixture. For the last 8 minutes of grilling, place eggplant slices on the rack alongside the chicken; turn once and brush occasionally with reserved soy sauce mixture. Transfer chicken and eggplant to cutting board; cool for 5 minutes and cut into cubes.

Toss chicken, eggplant, and cabbage with noodles. Sprinkle with cashews (if desired) and cilantro.

Nutrition facts per serving: 442 cal., 12 g total fat (2 g sat. fat), 108 mg chol., 646 mg sodium, 51 g carbo., 6 g fiber, 32 g pro. Daily values: 81% vit. A, 60% vit. C, 6% calcium, 28% iron

**Serving suggestion:**

*A simple and light dessert, such as chocolate-dipped fortune cookies and fruit sorbet, makes a refreshing finish to this meal.*

# smoky chicken wraps

**It's easy to get a grip on dinner when it's mesquite-smoked chicken all wrapped up in a tomato tortilla that's slathered with tomato-and-pine nut cream cheese. For variety, try other flavored tortillas, such as spinach. Plain works, too.**



**Prep:** 20 minutes **Marinate:** 15 minutes
**Grill:** 10 minutes **Makes** 4 servings

- **2** cups mesquite wood chips
- **12** ounces skinless, boneless chicken breast halves
- **1** tablespoon cooking oil
- **1** tablespoon Worcestershire sauce
- **1** teaspoon snipped fresh thyme
- **½** of an 8-ounce tub plain cream cheese
- **2** oil-packed dried tomatoes, drained and finely chopped
- **2** tablespoons chopped pine nuts or almonds (optional)
- **4** 8- or 9-inch tomato tortillas or plain flour tortillas
- **16** fresh basil leaves, cut into strips

At least 1 hour before grilling, soak wood chips in enough water to cover. Rinse chicken; pat dry. Place chicken in a shallow dish. For marinade, combine oil, Worcestershire sauce, thyme, and ¼ teaspoon pepper; pour over chicken. Cover; marinate at room temperature for 15 minutes.

In small bowl stir together cream cheese, dried tomatoes, and nuts (if desired). If necessary, stir in enough water to make of spreading consistency. Season to taste with salt and pepper; set aside. Wrap tortillas in heavy foil.

Drain wood chips. In a grill with a cover arrange preheated coals in an even layer. Sprinkle wood chips over coals. Place chicken on a lightly greased grill rack directly over medium-hot coals. Cover and grill 10 to 12 minutes or until chicken is tender and no longer pink, turning chicken and adding tortillas halfway through grilling.

Transfer chicken breasts to a cutting board; cool slightly and thinly slice. Spread the cream cheese mixture over tortillas; sprinkle with basil. Divide chicken among tortillas; roll up.

Nutrition facts per serving: 454 cal., 21 g total fat (6 g sat. fat), 77 mg chol., 798 mg sodium, 42 g carbo., 1 g fiber, 26 g pro. Daily values: 5% vit. A, 17% vit. C, 7% calcium, 21% iron

**Serving suggestion:**

*Toss together a simple salad of yellow or red pear tomatoes dressed with an herb vinaigrette to complete the meal.*

# southwest chicken salad

**Grilling lends sweet oranges a pleasing smoky flavor in this refreshingly different chicken salad. To make a side salad to serve with your favorite grilled meats, poultry, or fish, simply omit the chicken.**



- ½ cup bottled poppy seed salad dressing
- 1 small jalapeño pepper, seeded and finely chopped
- ½ teaspoon finely shredded orange peel
- 4 medium skinless, boneless chicken breast halves (about 1 pound total)
- 2 oranges, peeled and sliced ½ inch thick
- 1 red sweet pepper, seeded and quartered
- 8 cups torn mixed greens
- 1 small jicama, peeled and sliced into thin bite-size strips

**Serving suggestion:**

*A side for this main-dish salad is as simple as a stack of warmed flour tortillas.*

**Prep: 15 minutes Grill: 12 minutes Makes 4 servings**

In a small bowl combine dressing, jalapeño, and orange peel. Reserve all but 1 tablespoon dressing mixture. Rinse chicken; pat dry. Brush the chicken, orange slices, and sweet pepper with the 1 tablespoon dressing mixture. Grill the chicken, orange slices, and sweet pepper on the lightly greased rack of an uncovered grill directly over medium heat for 12 to 15 minutes or until chicken is tender and no longer pink, turning once. Transfer the chicken, orange slices, and sweet pepper to a cutting board; cool slightly. Cut chicken and sweet pepper into bite-size strips; quarter the orange slices.

Meanwhile, in a large salad bowl toss together the greens and jicama. Add the chicken, oranges, and sweet pepper to the salad bowl; drizzle with the reserved dressing mixture. Season to taste with black pepper.

Nutrition facts per serving: 339 cal., 18 g total fat (3 g sat. fat), 59 mg chol., 194 mg sodium, 22 g carbo., 3 g fiber, 24 g pro. Daily values: 26% vit. A, 147% vit. C, 5% calcium, 11% iron

# provençal grilled chicken & herbed penne

**Fresh grilled vegetables, fruity and fragrant olive oil, a very French blend of herbs, and fresh thyme that grows in abundance on the rocky hillsides of the south of France give this dish the flavor of Provence. Enjoy it with a glass of chilled white wine.**



**Start to finish: 25 minutes   Makes 4 servings**

- **8 ounces dried tomato or garlic and herb-flavored penne pasta or plain penne pasta**
- **4 medium skinless, boneless chicken breast halves (about 1 pound total)**
- **1 medium zucchini, halved lengthwise**
- **8 thick asparagus spears (8 to 10 ounces total), trimmed**
- **3 tablespoons olive oil**
- **1 tablespoon fines herbes or herbes de Provence, crushed**
- **1 tablespoon snipped fresh thyme**
- **½ cup finely shredded Asiago or Pecorino Romano cheese**

Cook pasta according to package directions. Meanwhile, rinse chicken; pat dry. Brush chicken, zucchini, and asparagus with 1 tablespoon of the oil; sprinkle all sides with fines herbes and ½ teaspoon salt.

Place the chicken in center of the lightly greased rack of an uncovered grill; place the zucchini and asparagus around chicken. Grill directly over medium heat for 12 to 15 minutes or until chicken is tender and no longer pink and vegetables are tender, turning once.

Transfer chicken and vegetables to cutting board; cool slightly. Cut chicken and zucchini into 1-inch cubes; slice asparagus into 1-inch-long pieces. Drain pasta; return to saucepan. Add chicken, vegetables, remaining oil, and thyme to pasta; toss well. Divide among 4 dinner plates; top with cheese and season with pepper.

Nutrition facts per serving: 480 cal., 17 g total fat (2 g sat. fat), 69 mg chol., 492 mg sodium, 45 g carbo., 4 g fiber, 35 g pro. Daily values: 7% vit. A, 20% vit. C, 15% calcium, 17% iron

### Serving suggestion:

*All this pasta dish needs is a crisp romaine or mesclun salad and some crusty French rolls.*

### culinary **cousins**

Fines herbs and herbes de Provence—both French herb blends—are interchangeable. Fines herbs is a quartet of chervil, chives, parsley, and tarragon. Herbes de Provence is a melange of basil, fennel, lavender, marjoram, rosemary, sage, savory, and thyme.

# sesame-ginger barbecued chicken

**This Asian-style barbecue sauce spiked with Oriental chili sauce is so good, you'll definitely want to warm up the extra and pass it at the table with the chicken. But watch closely—or the bowl may be empty by the time it gets to you!**



- **⅓ cup plum sauce or sweet-sour sauce**
- **¼ cup water**
- **3 tablespoons hoisin sauce**
- **1½ teaspoons sesame seed (toasted, if desired)**
- **1 clove garlic, minced**
- **1 teaspoon grated fresh ginger or ¼ teaspoon ground ginger**
- **¼ to ½ teaspoon Oriental chili sauce or several dashes bottled hot pepper sauce**
- **6 small skinless, boneless chicken breast halves and/or thighs (about 1½ pounds total)**

### Serving suggestion:

*Besides the extra sauce, serve this sweet-savory barbecued chicken with bottled sesame-vinaigrette dressed slaw—and Grilled Pineapple with Sugared Wontons (page 177) for dessert.*

**Prep: 10 minutes Grill: 12 minutes Makes 6 servings**

For sauce, in a small saucepan combine all of the ingredients except the chicken. Bring to boiling over medium heat, stirring frequently; reduce heat. Simmer, covered, for 3 minutes. Set aside.

Rinse chicken; pat dry. Grill chicken on the lightly greased rack of an uncovered grill directly over medium heat for 12 to 15 minutes or until tender and no longer pink, turning once and brushing with sauce once or twice during the last 5 minutes of grilling.

In a small saucepan heat the remaining sauce until bubbly; pass with chicken.

Nutrition facts per serving: 166 cal., 4 g total fat (1 g sat. fat), 59 mg chol., 216 mg sodium, 9 g carbo., 0 g fiber, 22 g pro. Daily values: 1% vit. A, 1% vit. C, 1% calcium, 5% iron

## it's **hot, hot, hot** (or not)

Here's a simple way to test the approximate temperature of your coals. Hold your hand over where the food will cook for as long as it is comfortable. The number of seconds you can hold it there gives you a clue.

| Number of seconds | Coal Temperature |
|---|---|
| 2 | High |
| 3 | Medium-high |
| 4 | Medium |
| 5 | Medium-low |
| 6 | Low |

# apple & grilled chicken salad

**Pick your favorite apples to make this salad. Either red or green apples work fine—just make sure they're a tart variety, such as Granny Smith, McIntosh, or Jonathan.**



- **⅓ cup apple jelly**
- **¼ cup horseradish mustard**
- **12 ounces skinless, boneless chicken breast halves (about 3 medium)**
- **4 cups mesclun or torn mixed greens**
- **2 tart medium apples, cored and sliced**
- **⅓ cup coarsely chopped walnuts (toasted, if desired)**
- **1 tablespoon cider vinegar**
- **1 tablespoon salad oil**

**Serving suggestion:**

*Warm corn muffins or corn bread is all that's needed to complete this main-dish salad meal.*

**Prep: 20 minutes Grill: 12 minutes Makes 4 servings**

In a small saucepan melt apple jelly over low heat. Remove from heat; stir in mustard. Reserve all but 2 tablespoons jelly mixture. Rinse chicken; pat dry. Grill chicken on the lightly greased rack of an uncovered grill directly over medium heat for 12 to 15 minutes or until tender and no longer pink, turning once and brushing occasionally with the 2 tablespoons jelly mixture during the last 5 minutes of grilling. Transfer chicken to a cutting board; cool slightly and bias-slice.

Meanwhile, toss the mesclun with the apples and walnuts. For dressing, stir together the reserved jelly mixture, vinegar, and oil. Divide the greens mixture among 4 dinner plates. Arrange chicken atop the greens; drizzle with the dressing.

Nutrition facts per serving: 307 cal., 13 g total fat (2 g sat. fat), 45 mg chol., 186 mg sodium, 30 g carbo., 2 g fiber, 19 g pro. Daily values: 2% vit. A, 11% vit. C, 3% calcium, 10% iron

# west indies chicken with grilled fruit

**Who says exotic has to be hard? This innovative, island-inspired, sweet-and-savory dish of grilled tropical fruit and chicken glossed with a spicy, herb-infused marmalade glaze is as easy as can be.**



**Prep: 15 minutes Grill: 12 minutes Makes 4 servings**

- 2 teaspoons finely shredded grapefruit or orange peel
- 3 tablespoons orange marmalade
- 2 teaspoons olive oil
- 1 tablespoon snipped fresh thyme
- 2½ teaspoons ground coriander
- ½ teaspoon hot Hungarian paprika or ⅛ teaspoon ground red pepper
- 1 small ruby red grapefruit
- 2 ripe, yet firm, kiwi fruit
- 2 medium ripe, yet firm, nectarines
- 2 ripe, yet firm, carambola (star fruit)
- 4 medium skinless, boneless chicken breast halves (about 1 pound total)

In a small bowl combine grapefruit peel, orange marmalade, oil, thyme, coriander, paprika, and ¼ teaspoon salt; set aside.

Peel and quarter grapefruit and kiwi fruit. Pit and quarter nectarines. Cut carambola into ½-inch-thick slices. Thread fruits on 4 metal skewers. Rinse chicken; pat dry. Grill chicken on the lightly greased rack of an uncovered grill directly over medium heat for 12 to 15 minutes or until chicken is tender and no longer pink, turning once. For the last 8 minutes of grilling, place fruit skewers on grill rack directly over medium heat. Brush fruit and chicken often with marmalade mixture; turn fruit once.

Nutrition facts per serving: 288 cal., 7 g total fat (1 g sat. fat), 59 mg chol., 192 mg sodium, 36 g carbo., 3 g fiber, 24 g pro. Daily values: 12% vit. A, 142% vit. C, 5% calcium, 11% iron

**Serving suggestion:**

*While the chicken and fruit are grilling, cook some rice or couscous for a side dish.*

# stuffed turkey tenderloins

**There's more than one way to stuff a turkey. Fresh spinach and tangy goat cheese make a melt-in-your-mouth filling in these turkey tenderloins. When sliced, the rosy-red, spicy crust on the meat yields to a juicy, tender interior.**



**Prep: 15 minutes Grill: 16 minutes Makes 4 servings**

- 2 8-ounce turkey breast tenderloins
- 2 cups chopped fresh spinach leaves
- 3 ounces semisoft goat cheese (chèvre) or feta cheese, crumbled (about 3/4 cup)
- 1/2 teaspoon black pepper
- 1 tablespoon olive oil
- 1 teaspoon paprika
- 1/2 teaspoon salt
- 1/8 to 1/4 teaspoon ground red pepper

Rinse turkey; pat dry. Make a pocket in each tenderloin by cutting lengthwise from one side almost to, but not through, the opposite side; set aside. In a bowl combine the spinach, cheese, and black pepper. Spoon spinach mixture into pockets. Tie 100% cotton kitchen string around each tenderloin in 3 or 4 places to hold in stuffing.

In small bowl combine oil, paprika, salt, and ground red pepper; brush evenly over tenderloins. Grill on the lightly greased rack of an uncovered grill directly over medium heat for 16 to 20 minutes or until turkey is tender and no longer pink in center of the thickest part; turn once. Remove and discard strings; slice tenderloins crosswise.

Nutrition facts per serving: 220 cal., 12 g total fat (4 g sat. fat), 68 mg chol., 458 mg sodium, 1 g carbo., 1 g fiber, 26 g pro. Daily values: 24% vit. A, 14% vit. C, 5% calcium, 13% iron

**Serving suggestion:**

*Fix up purchased mashed potatoes with your favorite fresh herb and serve the turkey and potatoes with slices of honeydew melon.*

# turkey burgers with fresh curry catsup

**America's favorite condiment goes haute cuisine! Plain old catsup gets a lift from fresh tomatoes, cilantro, and curry powder to dress up a burger flavored with ginger, garlic, and more curry. Lightly grilled pita bread fills in for a more ordinary bun.**



- **1 beaten egg**
- **¼ cup fine dry bread crumbs**
- **2 tablespoons snipped fresh cilantro**
- **2 teaspoons grated fresh ginger**
- **1 clove garlic, minced**
- **½ teaspoon salt**
- **½ teaspoon curry powder**
- **¼ teaspoon freshly ground black pepper**
- **1 pound ground raw turkey**
- **1 recipe Curry Catsup**
- **2 large pita bread rounds (optional)**

**Serving suggestion:**

*Serve these out-of-the-ordinary burgers with sweet-potato chips—found in the snack aisle of most supermarkets.*

**Prep: 20 minutes Grill: 14 minutes Makes 4 servings**

In a large bowl combine egg, bread crumbs, cilantro, ginger, garlic, salt, curry powder, and pepper. Add turkey and mix well. Form turkey mixture into four ¾-inch-thick patties. (If mixture is sticky, moisten hands with water.) Grill patties on the lightly greased rack of an uncovered grill directly over medium heat for 14 to 18 minutes or until juices run clear and no pink remains, turning once.

To serve, spoon the Curry Catsup over the burgers. (Or, lightly grill pita rounds on both sides until toasted, allowing 1 to 2 minutes per side. Cut rounds in half; place burger in each pita half and top with Curry Catsup.)

**Curry Catsup:** Chop 4 medium plum tomatoes. In medium saucepan combine tomatoes, ½ cup catsup, 3 tablespoons finely chopped onion, 2 tablespoons snipped fresh cilantro, and 2 teaspoons curry powder. Bring to boiling; reduce heat. Simmer, covered, for 5 minutes, stirring occasionally. Season to taste with salt and pepper.

Nutrition facts per serving: 407 cal., 11 g total fat (3 g sat. fat), 95 mg chol., 1,113 mg sodium, 52 g carbo., 2 g fiber, 24 g pro. Daily values: 10% vit. A, 33% vit. C, 8% calcium, 27% iron

# duck breast with lime sauce

**A casual cookout can be elegant, too. Grilled duck breast served with a fruity sauce and a garnish of fresh red raspberries makes beautiful company fare with no fuss.**



**Prep: 20 minutes Grill: 10 minutes Makes 4 servings**

- ½ cup currant jelly
- ¼ cup sweet or semi-dry white wine, such as Riesling or sauterne
- 1 tablespoon raspberry vinegar
- 1 teaspoon finely shredded lime peel
- 1 tablespoon lime juice
- ¼ teaspoon grated fresh ginger
- 1 tablespoon margarine or butter
- 4 skinless, boneless duck or chicken breast halves (about 1 pound total)
- 2 teaspoons olive oil
- Fresh red raspberries (optional)

In a small saucepan combine jelly, wine, vinegar, lime peel, lime juice, ginger, ⅛ teaspoon salt, and dash pepper. Bring just to boiling; reduce heat. Simmer, uncovered, about 12 minutes or until sauce is slightly thickened and reduced to ½ cup. Remove from heat; stir in margarine. Reserve all but ¼ cup of the jelly mixture.

Meanwhile, rinse duck breasts; pat dry. Brush oil over both sides of duck breasts. Grill duck on the lightly greased rack of an uncovered grill directly over medium heat for 10 to 12 minutes or until tender and no pink remains, turning once and brushing with the ¼ cup jelly mixture during the last 2 to 3 minutes of grilling. Serve duck with the reserved jelly mixture. Garnish with raspberries, if desired.

Nutrition facts per serving: 222 cal., 8 g total fat (2 g sat. fat), 22 mg chol., 124 mg sodium, 29 g carbo., 0 g fiber, 6 g pro. Daily values: 4% vit. A, 5% vit. C, 1% calcium, 8% iron

### fowl play

Despite its rich reputation, duck these days is being bred and raised to be both lean and moist. Duck is known for its distinctive flavor. Generally, older and heavier birds are stronger flavored and less tender. Most commercially raised ducks are fed a regulated diet and sold young to produce sweet and tender meat. Duck is available both fresh and frozen.

**Serving suggestion:**

*Round out this elegant duck dinner with steamed asparagus and whole wheat rolls with herbed butter.*

# fresh catches

# grilled rosemary trout with lemon butter

**Taste the delicious reason lemon and butter are the timeless, classic accompaniments to fish! This recipe is so simple you'll want to tote it along on your next fishing trip. Spicy Potato Slices (page 158) can be grilled alongside the fish.**



**Prep: 15 minutes Grill: 6 minutes Makes 4 servings**

- 4 teaspoons butter, softened
- 1 teaspoon finely shredded lemon peel
- 1 tablespoon finely chopped shallots or onion
- 2 fresh rainbow trout, pan dressed and boned (8 to 10 ounces each)*
- 1 tablespoon snipped fresh rosemary
- 1 tablespoon lemon juice
- 2 teaspoons olive oil
- 2 medium tomatoes, halved crosswise
- 1 tablespoon snipped fresh parsley

In a small bowl stir together the butter, lemon peel, and half of the shallots; season with salt and coarsely ground black pepper. Set aside.

Rinse fish; pat dry. Spread each fish open. Place fish skin sides down. Rub remaining shallots and the rosemary onto fish; sprinkle with additional salt and pepper and drizzle with lemon juice and oil. Grill fish, skin sides down, on the lightly greased rack of an uncovered grill directly over medium heat for 6 to 8 minutes or until fish flakes easily when tested with a fork.

Meanwhile, place tomatoes, cut sides up, on grill rack; dot each with ¼ teaspoon of the butter mixture. Grill for 5 minutes or until tomatoes are heated through. Remove fish and tomatoes from the grill. Cut each fish in half lengthwise. In a small saucepan melt remaining butter mixture; serve with fish and tomatoes. Sprinkle fish with parsley.

Nutrition facts per serving: 206 cal., 10 g total fat (3 g sat. fat), 75 mg chol., 109 mg sodium, 4 g carbo., 1 g fiber, 24 g pro. Daily values: 13% vit. A, 31% vit. C, 7% calcium, 17% iron

**Note: A pan-dressed fish has had the scales and internal organs removed; often the head, fins, and tail also have been removed.*

**Serving suggestion:**

*This classic trout-and-potatoes dinner calls for an equally classic dessert: Try Nectarine-Raspberry Crisp (page 171).*

# sea bass with black bean & avocado relish

**This island-style fish dish draws on the best of Cuba—the land itself (black beans, avocado, and lime) and the water that surrounds it (sea bass). Serve it with a splash of fruit juice, such as pineapple, mango, or papaya, stirred with sparkling water.**



- **4 4- to 5-ounce fresh sea bass fillets, ¾ to 1 inch thick**
- **2 tablespoons snipped fresh cilantro**
- **2 tablespoons snipped fresh oregano**
- **½ teaspoon finely shredded lime peel**
- **2 tablespoons lime juice**
- **1 tablespoon olive oil**
- **¼ to ½ teaspoon bottled hot pepper sauce**
- **1 clove garlic, minced**
- **1 15-ounce can black beans, rinsed and drained**
- **1 avocado, seeded, peeled, and diced**

**Serving suggestion:**

*If you want a little something extra on the plate, consider sweet and spicy Honey-Glazed Bananas (page 162).*

**Prep: 15 minutes Grill: 4 to 6 minutes per ½-inch thickness**

**Makes 4 servings**

Rinse fish; pat dry. Measure thickness of fish; set aside. In a small bowl stir together cilantro, oregano, lime peel, lime juice, oil, pepper sauce, and garlic. Place 2 tablespoons cilantro mixture in a medium bowl. Add beans and avocado; toss lightly to coat. Cover and refrigerate while cooking fish.

Brush remaining cilantro mixture over fish. Grill fish on the lightly greased rack of an uncovered grill directly over medium heat until fish flakes easily when tested with a fork, turning once. (Allow 4 to 6 minutes per ½-inch thickness of fish.) Serve with bean mixture.

Nutrition facts per serving: 303 cal., 15 g total fat (2 g sat. fat), 47 mg chol., 348 mg sodium, 20 g carbo., 6 g fiber, 29 g pro. Daily values: 9% vit. A, 16% vit. C, 4% calcium, 13% iron

# grilled swordfish with spicy tomato sauce

**This vibrant and fresh example of the best of fusion cooking combines two popular Sicilian foods, swordfish and a spicy, fresh tomato sauce, with couscous, a North African favorite.**



**Prep: 15 minutes Grill: 8 minutes Makes 4 servings**

- **4 fresh swordfish steaks, 1 inch thick (about 1¼ pounds)**
- **4 teaspoons cooking oil**
- **¼ cup chopped onion**
- **1 small serrano or jalapeño pepper, seeded and finely chopped**
- **½ teaspoon bottled minced garlic**
- **½ teaspoon ground turmeric**
- **¼ teaspoon ground coriander**
- **1½ cups chopped plum tomatoes**
- **1 tablespoon snipped fresh cilantro**
- **Hot cooked couscous (optional)**

Rinse fish; pat dry. Drizzle 2 teaspoons of the oil over swordfish. Sprinkle with ¼ teaspoon each of salt and black pepper. Grill on the lightly greased rack of an uncovered grill directly over medium heat for 8 to 12 minutes or until fish flakes easily when tested with a fork; turn once.

Meanwhile, for the spicy tomato sauce, in a medium skillet heat the remaining oil. Add onion, serrano or jalapeño pepper, garlic, turmeric, and coriander; cook about 2 minutes or until onions are tender. Stir in tomatoes and ¼ teaspoon salt; cook 2 to 3 minutes or until tomatoes are just tender. Remove from heat; stir in cilantro. Serve spicy tomato sauce over fish. If desired, serve with couscous.

Nutrition facts per serving: 237 cal., 11 g total fat (2 g sat. fat), 56 mg chol., 402 mg sodium, 5 g carbo., 1 g fiber, 29 g pro. Daily values: 9% vit. A, 39% vit. C, 1% calcium, 11% iron

## Serving suggestion:

*Start this elegant swordfish dinner with a simple appetizer of Italian black or green olives and pieces of crisp lavosh.*

## fish-grilling **101**

Fillets of fish can break apart easily, so it helps to place them on foil or in a grill basket for grilling. To keep the fish from sticking, lightly brush the foil or basket with cooking oil before adding the fish. To avoid the fish poaching in its own juices during grilling, cut slits in the foil to allow the juices to run through. Firmer-textured fish cut into steaks—such as salmon, halibut, and swordfish—are grilled easily on a lightly greased grill rack.

# wasabi-glazed whitefish with vegetable slaw

**Though its presence in this recipe is subtle, fans of fiery wasabi—the bright-green Japanese horseradish condiment—will notice its head-clearing heat. Wasabi is found in powdered or paste form in Japanese markets or in larger supermarkets.**



**Prep: 15 minutes Grill: 6 minutes Makes 4 servings**

- 4 4-ounce fresh white-fleshed skinless fish fillets, about ¾ inch thick*
- 2 tablespoons light soy sauce
- ¼ teaspoon wasabi powder or 1 tablespoon prepared horseradish
- 1 teaspoon toasted sesame oil
- ½ teaspoon sugar
- 1 medium zucchini, coarsely shredded (about 1⅓ cups)
- 1 cup sliced radishes
- 1 cup fresh pea pods
- 3 tablespoons snipped fresh chives
- 3 tablespoons rice vinegar

Rinse fish; pat dry. In small bowl combine soy sauce, wasabi powder, ½ teaspoon of the sesame oil, and ¼ teaspoon of the sugar. Brush soy mixture over fish. Grill fish on the lightly greased rack of an uncovered grill directly over medium heat for 6 to 9 minutes or until fish flakes easily when tested with a fork, turning after 4 minutes.

Meanwhile, for vegetable slaw, in medium bowl combine the zucchini, radishes, pea pods, and 2 tablespoons of the chives. Stir together the remaining sesame oil, remaining sugar, and vinegar. Drizzle over the zucchini mixture; toss to combine. Sprinkle remaining chives over fish. Serve fish with vegetable slaw.

Nutrition facts per serving: 141 cal., 3 g total fat (1 g sat. fat), 60 mg chol., 363 mg sodium, 6 g carbo., 1 g fiber, 24 g pro. Daily values: 3% vit. A, 46% vit. C, 3% calcium, 10% iron

**Note: Use whitefish, sea bass, orange roughy, or any other similar fish fillets.*

**Serving suggestion:**

*Finish this dinner with Grilled Pineapple with Sugared Wontons (page 177).*

# grilled tuna with wilted spinach

**Tuna bears watching as it cooks because it easily can dry out. Here, a beautiful bed of tiny grape tomatoes and fresh spinach is quick-cooked in a skillet on the grill right next to the tuna—so you can keep your fish under a watchful eye.**



- **1¼ pounds fresh skinless tuna fillets, about ¾ inch thick**
- **3 tablespoons balsamic vinegar**
- **1 tablespoon olive oil**
- **¼ teaspoon garlic pepper**
- **1 medium red onion, sliced ¼ inch thick**
- **2 cups grape tomatoes or cherry tomatoes, halved**
- **6 cups torn fresh spinach or torn mixed greens**
- **2 tablespoons water**

**Serving suggestion:**

*Toss hot couscous with some toasted pine nuts and fresh herbs for a delicious accompaniment.*

**Prep: 15 minutes Marinate: 5 minutes**
**Grill: 6 minutes Makes 4 servings**

Rinse fish; pat dry. Cut fish into 4 portions. Lightly sprinkle with salt and pepper; place in shallow dish. In small mixing bowl stir together the vinegar, oil, garlic pepper, and ¼ teaspoon salt. Pour 2 tablespoons of the vinegar mixture over fish. Cover and marinate at room temperature for 5 minutes. Drain fish, reserving marinade. Grill fish and onion slices on lightly greased rack of an uncovered grill directly over medium heat for 6 to 9 minutes or until fish flakes easily when tested with a fork, turning and brushing with reserved marinade after 4 minutes.

While the fish is cooking, in a large heavy skillet* toss together the tomatoes, spinach, and water. Place skillet on grill rack directly over medium heat. Cook 3 to 4 minutes or until spinach begins to wilt, stirring occasionally. Transfer spinach mixture to serving platter; place fish and onion slices atop. Drizzle with remaining vinegar mixture.

Nutrition facts per serving: 299 cal., 11 g total fat (2 g sat. fat), 59 mg chol., 315 mg sodium, 10 g carbo., 3 g fiber, 39 g pro. Daily values: 134% vit. A, 58% vit. C, 6% calcium, 26% iron

**Note: The heat from the grill will blacken the outside of the skillet, so use a cast-iron or old skillet.*

# minty grilled halibut with yellow squash

**When you're truly pressed for time, but still crave something light and healthy, try this delicious fish. Flavored with fresh basil and mint and served with smoky, grilled summer squash, it's ready from start to finish in about 20 minutes!**



**Prep: 15 minutes Grill: 8 minutes Makes 4 servings**

Rinse fish; pat dry. In a small bowl whisk together the lemon juice, oil, and garlic. Reserve 3 tablespoons of the mixture. Brush remaining lemon juice mixture on fish and the cut sides of the squash. Lightly sprinkle fish and squash with salt and pepper. Grill fish on the lightly greased rack of an uncovered grill directly over medium heat for 8 to 12 minutes or until fish flakes easily when tested with a fork, turning once. During the last 5 to 6 minutes of grilling, grill the squash until just tender, turning once.

Meanwhile, stir basil and mint into the reserved lemon juice mixture.

Transfer the squash to a cutting board; cool slightly and slice ⅛ inch to ¼ inch thick. Place squash on a serving platter; drizzle with some of the basil mixture. Top with fish; drizzle with the remaining basil mixture.

Nutrition facts per serving: 233 cal., 10 g total fat (1 g sat. fat), 46 mg chol., 112 mg sodium, 5 g carbo., 1 g fiber, 30 g pro. Daily values: 8% vit. A, 19% vit. C, 7% calcium, 11% iron

- **1¼ to 1½ pounds fresh halibut or salmon steaks, 1 inch thick**
- **¼ cup lemon juice**
- **2 tablespoons olive oil**
- **3 cloves garlic, minced**
- **2 medium yellow summer squash or zucchini, halved lengthwise**
- **2 tablespoons finely snipped fresh basil**
- **1 tablespoon snipped fresh mint**

### Serving suggestion:

*Serve this speedy entrée with chewy Italian bread and follow it up with strawberries tossed with lemon juice and sugar and sprinkled with freshly ground black pepper.*

# dilly salmon fillets

**A quick, dill-infused, Dijon-flavored mayonnaise caps off these Scandinavian-style salmon fillets. For a built-in salad and extra freshness, serve them on a bed of shredded cucumber.**



- **4 6-ounce fresh skinless salmon fillets, ½ to ¾ inch thick**
- **3 tablespoons lemon juice**
- **2 tablespoons snipped fresh dill**
- **2 tablespoons mayonnaise or salad dressing**
- **2 teaspoons Dijon-style mustard**
- **Dash freshly ground black pepper**

**Serving suggestion:**

*Fill out this flavorful salmon dinner with Jasmine-Mint Tea Rice with Peas (page 159).*

**Prep: 15 minutes Marinate: 10 minutes**
**Grill: 5 minutes Makes 4 servings**

Rinse fish; pat dry and place in a shallow dish. In a small bowl combine the lemon juice and 1 tablespoon of the dill; pour over fish and marinate at room temperature for 10 minutes. Meanwhile, in a small bowl stir together the remaining dill, the mayonnaise, mustard, and pepper; set aside.

In a grill with a cover arrange preheated coals around drip pan. Test for medium heat above pan. Place the fish on the lightly greased grill rack over the drip pan. Cover and grill for 3 minutes. Turn fish; spread the mayonnaise mixture atop the fish. Cover and grill 2 to 6 minutes more or until fish flakes easily when tested with a fork.

Nutrition facts per serving: 211 cal., 11 g total fat (2 g sat. fat), 35 mg chol., 204 mg sodium, 1 g carbo., 0 g fiber, 25 g pro. Daily values: 4% vit. A, 8% vit. C, 1% calcium, 7% iron

# red snapper with fresh herb-pecan crust

**Butter, chopped pecans, fresh herbs, and a touch of lemon and garlic make a toasty crust on this meaty grilled red snapper. Instead of Italian parsley, you can substitute your favorite herb. It's terrific on fresh walleye, too!**



- **4 5- or 6-ounce red snapper fillets with skin**
- **2 tablespoons margarine or butter, softened**
- **⅓ cup finely chopped pecans**
- **2 tablespoons fine dry bread crumbs**
- **1 teaspoon finely shredded lemon peel**
- **2 garlic cloves, minced**
- **1 tablespoon snipped fresh Italian parsley**
- **¼ teaspoon salt**
- **⅛ teaspoon black pepper**
- **Dash ground red pepper**
- **Lemon wedges (optional)**

**Serving suggestion:**

*A bed of grilled zucchini and summer squash slices makes a pretty presentation for these fillets—or try a side of Grilled Corn Relish (page 169) and sourdough bread.*

**Prep: 15 minutes Grill: 4 to 6 minutes per ½-inch thickness**
**Makes 4 servings**

Rinse fish; pat dry. Measure thickness of fish; set aside. In a small bowl combine margarine, pecans, bread crumbs, lemon peel, garlic, the 1 tablespoon parsley, salt, black pepper, and red pepper. Place fish, skin side down, on the greased rack of an uncovered grill directly over medium coals. Spoon pecan mixture on top of fillets; spread slightly. Grill fish 4 to 6 minutes per ½-inch thickness, or until fish flakes easily with a fork. Transfer to a serving platter with a wide spatula. Sprinkle fish with additional snipped parsley and serve with lemon wedges, if desired.

Nutrition facts per serving: 268 cal., 14 g total fat (2 g sat. fat), 52 mg chol., 287 mg sodium, 7 g carbo., .8 g fiber, 30 g pro. Daily values: 7% vit. A, 4% vit. C, 4% calcium, 4% iron

## direct versus indirect

Direct grilling means food is placed on the rack directly over the coals. This method is often used for fast-cooking foods such as burgers, steaks, boneless chicken, fish, and seafood. Indirect grilling means a covered grill acts as an oven. A disposable drip pan is placed in the center of the charcoal grate and hot coals are arranged around it. This method is used for slower-cooking foods, such as roasts or bone-in poultry. Because of their speed, most of the recipes in this book call for direct grilling. See the grilling charts on pages 178–181 for timings.

# scallop brochettes

**A little bit sweet, a little bit tangy, these seafood brochettes, soaked in a simple marinade of sherry, mustard, honey, and soy sauce, can be made with scallops, shrimp, or a combination of both.**



**Prep: 15 minutes Marinate: 30 minutes**
**Grill: 6 minutes Makes 4 servings**

- 1 pound sea scallops and/or peeled and deveined shrimp
- 2 tablespoons cooking oil
- 2 tablespoons dry sherry
- 2 tablespoons stone-ground mustard
- 1 tablespoon honey
- 1½ teaspoons soy sauce

Halve large scallops (you should have about 20 pieces). Place scallops in a plastic bag set in a shallow dish. For marinade, in a small bowl combine oil, sherry, mustard, honey, and soy sauce. Pour over the scallops. Close bag; marinate in the refrigerator for 30 minutes.

Drain the scallops, discarding the marinade. Thread scallops on long metal skewers. (If using scallops and shrimp, thread a scallop in the "curl" of each shrimp.) Grill on the lightly greased rack of an uncovered grill directly over medium heat for 6 to 8 minutes or until scallops are opaque; turn once.

Nutrition facts per serving: 119 cal., 5 g total fat (1 g saturated fat), 34 mg chol., 284 mg sodium, 4 g carb., 0 g fiber, 15 g pro. Daily values: 6% calcium, 13% iron

**Serving suggestion:**

*Serve these seafood brochettes on a bed of cold rice vermicelli that has been tossed with a little toasted sesame oil, rice vinegar, and shredded carrots.*

# rosemary-orange shrimp kabobs

**Bacon-wrapped shrimp sounds decadent, but it can be everyday fare when you use light turkey bacon. Here, the bacon gives the shrimp a subtle smokiness, and a brushed-on herbed orange juice adds a pleasing sweetness.**



**Prep:** 20 minutes **Grill:** 8 minutes **Makes** 4 servings

Peel and devein shrimp, leaving tails intact. Rinse shrimp; pat dry. Wrap each shrimp in a half slice of bacon. Alternately thread shrimp and sweet pepper pieces on long metal skewers. In small bowl combine 1 teaspoon of the orange peel, the orange juice, and rosemary. Brush over kabobs.

Grill kabobs on the lightly greased rack of an uncovered grill directly over medium heat for 8 to 10 minutes or until bacon is crisp and shrimp turn pink, turning once.

Meanwhile, in a medium saucepan stir together the remaining peel, cooked rice, and beans; heat through. Serve with shrimp and peppers.

Nutrition facts per serving: 310 cal., 7 g total fat (2 g sat. fat), 149 mg chol., 563 mg sodium, 36 g carbo., 2 g fiber, 26 g pro. Daily values: 20% vit. A, 139% vit. C, 5% calcium, 29% iron

## a different kind of **orange**

Blood oranges, also called sanguines or Moro oranges, are becoming increasingly available—and that's a good thing. Sweeter and juicier than most oranges, they get their name from their mottled, deep-red flesh and blushing-red skin. They're wonderful for eating out of hand, and when used in a marinade, impart a rosy hue to foods.

- **1 pound large fresh shrimp in shells (about 16 shrimp)**
- **8 slices turkey bacon, halved crosswise**
- **2 red and/or yellow sweet peppers, cut into 1-inch pieces**
- **2 teaspoons finely shredded orange or blood orange peel**
- **2 tablespoons orange or blood orange juice**
- **2 teaspoons snipped fresh rosemary**
- **2 cups hot cooked rice**
- **1 cup cooked or canned black beans, rinsed and drained**

**Serving suggestion:**

*Follow these orange-herb-infused shrimp kabobs with coffee-flavored ice cream and chocolate-sauce sundaes.*

# garden variety grilling

# southwestern black bean cakes with guacamole

**These spicy bean cakes are finger foods that are filling enough to make a meal. They're flavored with a chipotle—a dried, smoked jalapeño pepper—that comes in adobo sauce, a Mexican melange of ground chili peppers, herbs, and vinegar.**



**Prep: 20 minutes Grill: 8 minutes Makes 4 servings**

- 2 slices whole wheat bread, torn
- 3 tablespoons fresh cilantro
- 2 cloves garlic
- 1 15-ounce can black beans, rinsed and drained
- 1 7-ounce can chipotle peppers in adobo sauce
- 1 teaspoon ground cumin
- 1 egg
- ½ of a medium avocado, seeded and peeled
- 1 tablespoon lime juice
- 1 small plum tomato, chopped

Place torn bread in a food processor bowl or blender container. Cover and process or blend until bread resembles coarse crumbs; transfer to a large bowl and set aside. Place cilantro and garlic in the food processor bowl or blender container; cover and process or blend until finely chopped. Add beans, 1 of the chipotle peppers, 1 to 2 teaspoons of the adobo sauce (reserve remaining peppers and sauce for another use), and cumin; process or blend using on/off pulses until beans are coarsely chopped and mixture begins to pull away from sides. Add mixture to bread crumbs in bowl. Add egg; mix well and shape into four ½-inch-thick patties.

Grill patties on the lightly greased rack of an uncovered grill directly over medium heat for 8 to 10 minutes or until patties are heated through, turning once.

Meanwhile, for guacamole, in small bowl mash avocado. Stir in lime juice; season with salt and pepper. Serve patties with guacamole and tomato.

Nutrition facts per serving: 178 cal., 7 g total fat (1 g sat. fat), 53 mg chol., 487 mg sodium, 25 g carbo., 9 g fiber, 11 g pro. Daily values: 9% vit. A, 12% vit. C, 7% calcium, 16% iron

**Serving suggestion:**

*For burger baskets, place the bean cakes on a bed of purchased baked tortilla chips in a lined basket or bowl and garnish with orange wedges.*

# tomato ravioli with grilled portobellos & spinach

**Rosy-hued purchased sun-dried tomato ravioli are dotted with a fresh green duo of spinach and sweet basil. Slices of smoky, garlic-infused grilled portobello mushrooms are substantial enough you won't notice the absence of meat.**



- **2 tablespoons olive oil**
- **2 garlic cloves, minced**
- **4 to 5 large portobello mushrooms (about 1 pound total), stems removed**
- **1 9-ounce package refrigerated cheese-filled sun-dried-tomato-flavored ravioli**
- **4 cups torn fresh spinach**
- **1 tablespoon snipped fresh basil**
- **¼ cup grated Parmesan cheese**
- **¼ teaspoon freshly ground black pepper**
- **Grated Parmesan cheese (optional)**

**Serving suggestion:**

*Warm up wedges of focaccia on the grill to nibble alongside this pretty pasta dish.*

**Prep: 15 minutes Grill: 10 minutes Makes 4 servings**

Combine 1 tablespoon of the oil and the garlic. Lightly brush rounded side of mushrooms with garlic-oil mixture; sprinkle lightly with salt and pepper. Grill mushrooms on the rack of an uncovered grill directly over medium coals for 10 to 12 minutes or until slightly softened, turning once. Slice the mushrooms into bite-size pieces.

Meanwhile, cook the ravioli in boiling, lightly salted water according to package directions. For the last 1 minute of cooking, add spinach to boiling pasta water; drain. Place ravioli and spinach in a large bowl; add mushrooms. Toss with remaining oil, basil, the ¼ cup Parmesan cheese, and the ¼ teaspoon freshly ground black pepper. If desired, serve with additional grated Parmesan cheese.

Nutrition facts per serving: 336 cal., 18 g total fat (7 g sat. fat), 61 mg chol., 500 mg sodium, 31 g carbo., 3 g fiber, 16 g pro. Daily values: 40% vit. A, 35% vit. C, 25% calcium, 31% iron

### bella **portobello!**

Meaty portobello mushrooms are the mature form of the crimino mushroom, a brown variation of the white button mushroom. Portobellos are great for the grill—simply brush them with olive oil and garlic. The grilled result can be eaten like a steak, sliced and tossed with pasta, rolled in a tortilla with grilled red peppers, or slipped between slices of grilled focaccia or bread.

# tandoori sweet potatoes with raita & pilau

**Sweet potatoes aren't just for Thanksgiving anymore. They're great on the grill in this vegetarian entrée that's spiced with curry butter and served with a cooling yogurt sauce and fruit-and-nut-studded pilau.**



**Prep: 25 minutes Grill: 15 minutes Makes 4 servings**

- 2 large or 4 small sweet potatoes or yams (about 1½ pounds total)
- 3 tablespoons butter, melted
- 1 to 2 tablespoons curry powder or garam masala (page 115)
- 1 small onion, chopped
- 1 cup basmati rice
- 2 cups water
- ⅓ cup snipped dried apricots or assorted dried fruit
- ¼ cup slivered almonds, toasted
- 1 8-ounce carton plain yogurt
- 1 tablespoon snipped fresh cilantro

Peel sweet potatoes and cut into ½-inch-thick slices. In a small bowl stir together the melted butter and curry powder. Brush butter mixture onto both sides of the sweet potato slices, reserving any remaining butter mixture. Place the sweet potatoes on the rack of a grill with a cover directly over medium heat; cover and grill for 15 to 18 minutes or until tender, turning occasionally.

Meanwhile, for the pilau, in a large saucepan heat remaining butter mixture over medium heat. Add onion; cook about 3 minutes or until tender. Add the rice; cook and stir for 3 to 4 minutes more or until the rice begins to brown. Carefully add the water. Heat to boiling; reduce heat. Simmer, covered, about 15 minutes or until the liquid is absorbed and the rice is tender. Remove from heat. Stir in apricots, almonds, and salt and pepper to taste. Cover and let stand for 5 minutes.

For the raita, in a small bowl combine the yogurt and cilantro; season with salt and pepper.

Serve the sweet potatoes with the pilau and raita.

Nutrition facts per serving: 499 cal., 14 g total fat (6 g sat. fat), 27 mg chol., 216 mg sodium, 83 g carbo., 8 g fiber, 11 g pro. Daily values: 306% vit. A, 56% vit. C, 16% calcium, 26% iron

**Serving suggestion:**

*If it's spicy curry powder you crave, cool the fire after dinner with a few scoops of mango sorbet.*

# saffron pilaf with grilled vegetables

**Similar to paella—Spain's national dish—this sunny-colored saffron rice dish is bursting with flavor, but from a rainbow of grilled vegetables instead of the standard shrimp and meat. Serve it with a hearty red wine.**



**Prep: 20 minutes Grill: 10 minutes Makes 4 servings**

- 1 cup jasmine, basmati, or wild-pecan long grain rice
- 1 14½-ounce can vegetable broth
- ¼ cup water
- ⅛ teaspoon saffron threads or dash ground saffron*
- 2 tablespoons olive oil
- ½ teaspoon bottled minced garlic
- 1 red sweet pepper, seeded and quartered
- 1 large zucchini, halved lengthwise
- 1 eggplant, sliced ½ inch thick
- 1 ounce herbed semi-soft goat cheese (chèvre), crumbled
- 2 tablespoons coarsely chopped hazelnuts or pecans, toasted

In a large saucepan combine rice, vegetable broth, water, and saffron. Heat to boiling; reduce heat. Simmer, covered, about 15 minutes or until rice is tender and liquid is absorbed; keep warm.

Meanwhile, in a small bowl combine oil and garlic; brush over sweet pepper, zucchini, and eggplant. Grill vegetables on the lightly greased rack of an uncovered grill directly over medium heat about 10 minutes or until tender, turning once. Season with salt and pepper to taste.

Transfer vegetables to cutting board; cool slightly. Cut vegetables into bite-size pieces; stir into cooked rice. Top with goat cheese and nuts.

Nutrition facts per serving: 333 cal., 12 g total fat (2 g sat. fat), 7 mg chol., 443 mg sodium, 48 g carbo., 5 g fiber, 9 g pro. Daily values: 5% vit. A, 40% vit. C, 4% calcium, 20% iron

*Note: You may substitute ¼ teaspoon turmeric for the saffron.*

**Serving suggestion:**

*Start an outdoor feast featuring this Spanish-style pilaf with tapas-style appetizers including olives, grilled vegetables, and cubes of piquant cheese.*

# grilled gazpacho medley open-faced sandwich

**Stay as cool as a cucumber with this hearty sandwich featuring the flavors of the cold soup, gazpacho. Tomatoes, garlic, cucumbers, and jalapeños get mixed with black beans, then scooped into grilled French bread "bowls" and topped with cheese.**



- **1 medium cucumber, seeded and chopped**
- **1 cup cooked or canned black beans, rinsed and drained**
- **¼ cup snipped fresh cilantro**
- **1 tablespoon olive oil**
- **2 tablespoons cider vinegar**
- **1 clove garlic, minced**
- **1 pickled jalapeño pepper, finely chopped**
- **½ to 1 teaspoon chili powder**
- **3 large tomatoes, halved**
- **1 large sweet onion (such as Vidalia), sliced ½ inch thick**
- **1 loaf French bread**
- **1 cup shredded cheddar cheese**

**Serving suggestion:**

*One Mexican-inspired dish deserves another: Satisfy sweet tooths with Grilled Chocolate-Raspberry Burritos (page 173).*

**Prep: 20 minutes Grill: 13 minutes Makes 6 servings**

In a medium bowl combine the cucumber, beans, cilantro, oil, vinegar, garlic, jalapeño, chili powder, and salt and pepper to taste. Set aside.

Place the tomatoes and onion slices on the lightly greased rack of a grill with a cover directly over medium heat; grill, uncovered, for 12 to 15 minutes or until lightly charred, turning onion slices once. Transfer vegetables to a cutting board; cool slightly and coarsely chop. Add chopped vegetables to the cucumber mixture; toss to combine.

Meanwhile, halve the French bread lengthwise. Cut each bread half crosswise into 3 pieces. Using a fork, hollow out the bread pieces slightly. Grill the bread pieces, cut sides down, about 1 minute or until toasted. Spoon the bean mixture into the bread pieces; sprinkle sandwiches with cheddar cheese. Place the sandwiches on the grill rack, filled sides up; close lid and grill for 1 to 2 minutes or until cheese is melted.

Nutrition facts per serving: 329 cal., 11 g total fat (5 g sat. fat), 20 mg chol., 634 mg sodium, 46 g carbo., 3 g fiber, 14 g pro. Daily values: 12% vit. A, 19% vit. C, 17% calcium, 18% iron

# spaghetti squash with grilled plum tomatoes

**If you've never tried spaghetti squash, here's a delightful way to get acquainted. The cooked flesh of this creamy-yellow squash separates into toothsome, spaghetti-like strands. What better way to eat it than topped with a grilled-tomato sauce?**



**Prep: 15 minutes Microwave: 10 minutes**
**Grill: 10 minutes Makes 4 to 6 servings**

- 1 2½-pound spaghetti squash, halved lengthwise and seeded
- 2 tablespoons water
- 4 teaspoons olive oil
- 1 teaspoon dried Italian seasoning
- ½ teaspoon salt
- ¼ teaspoon pepper
- ½ cup finely shredded Parmesan cheese
- 4 medium red and/or yellow plum tomatoes, quartered
- 2 tablespoons snipped fresh basil

Place squash, cut sides down, in a microwave-safe 2-quart rectangular baking dish; add the water. Prick skin all over with a fork. Cover with vented plastic wrap. Microwave on 100% power (high) about 10 minutes or until squash is tender. Let squash stand for 5 minutes.

Combine oil, Italian seasoning, salt, and pepper. Using fork, remove pulp from squash shells, separating it into strands. Transfer to bowl; toss with 2 teaspoons of the oil mixture and the Parmesan cheese. Fold a 36×18-inch piece of heavy foil in half to make a double thickness of foil that measures 18×18 inches. Place squash mixture in center of foil. Bring up opposite edges of foil and seal with double fold. Fold remaining edges to completely enclose the squash mixture, leaving space for steam to build. Grill squash packet on the rack of an uncovered grill directly over medium heat for 10 minutes, turning once. Toss tomatoes with remaining oil mixture. For last 5 minutes of grilling, place tomatoes on grill rack beside packet. Grill tomatoes just until tender, turning once. Transfer tomatoes to cutting board; cool slightly and chop. Spoon over squash; sprinkle with basil.

Nutrition facts per serving: 133 cal., 8 g total fat (1 g sat. fat), 10 mg chol., 447 mg sodium, 9 g carbo., 2 g fiber, 6 g pro. Daily values: 6% vit. A, 25% vit. C, 12% calcium, 5% iron

## Serving suggestion:

*Round out this healthy vegetarian meal with Piquant Grilled Broccoli & Olives (page 165) and grilled whole wheat Italian country bread.*

# grilled sicilian-style pizza

**Sicilians like their escarole—a mild, leafy kind of endive—sautéed with lots of olive oil and served with chewy bread to sop up the juices. For maximum flavor in this grilled adaptation of that idea, use the tangy Italian cheese, Pecorino Romano.**



- **1 16-ounce Italian bread shell (Boboli)**
- **2 plum tomatoes, thinly sliced**
- **1 large yellow or red tomato, thinly sliced**
- **4 ounces fresh mozzarella or buffalo mozzarella cheese, thinly sliced**
- **⅓ cup halved, pitted kalamata olives**
- **1 tablespoon olive oil**
- **1 cup coarsely chopped escarole or curly endive**
- **¼ cup shredded Pecorino Romano or Parmesan cheese (1 ounce)**

### Serving suggestion:

*Finish this meal-in-one with a flourish. Serve with purchased biscotti and a little sweet wine—such as Vin Santo—or espresso or cappuccino for dipping.*

**Prep: 20 minutes Grill: 8 minutes Makes 4 servings**

Top bread shell with tomatoes, mozzarella cheese, and olives. Drizzle oil over all. Fold a 24×18-inch piece of heavy foil in half lengthwise. Place on foil, turning edges of foil up to edge of pizza.

In a grill with a cover arrange preheated coals around a drip pan for indirect grilling. Test for medium heat above pan. Place pizza on the grill rack over the drip pan. Cover and grill about 8 minutes or until pizza is heated through, topping with escarole the last 2 minutes of grilling. To serve, sprinkle cheese and freshly ground black pepper over pizza.

Nutrition facts per serving: 459 cal., 19 g total fat (4 g sat. fat), 26 mg chol., 893 mg sodium, 54 g carbo., 3 g fiber, 24 g pro. Daily values:12% vit. A, 14% vit. C, 31% calcium, 18% iron

### **fresh** is best

They may have the same last name, but the similarity ends there. Fresh mozzarella—made from whole milk—has a much softer texture and sweeter, more delicate flavor than regular mozzarella, which is made in low-fat and nonfat versions and is aged to give it a longer shelf life. Fresh mozzarella, usually packaged in whey or water and shaped into irregular balls, must be eaten within a few days of purchase. It's available in Italian markets and cheese shops and increasingly, in many supermarkets.

# simple sides

# grilled antipasto skewers

**Not really onions at all—but sometimes called wild onions—cipollini are actually the bittersweet bulbs of the grape hyacinth. Fresh cipollini are available mostly in late summer and fall. If you can't find them at your supermarket, check at Italian markets.**



**Prep: 25 minutes Grill: 8 minutes Makes 6 servings**

- ⅓ cup balsamic vinegar
- 1 6½-ounce jar marinated artichoke hearts
- 1 medium red sweet pepper, cut into 1-inch pieces
- 1 medium yellow sweet pepper, cut into 1-inch pieces
- 8 small whole or 4 medium cipollini, halved, or 8 pearl onions
- 8 large crimini or button mushrooms, stems removed
- 2 ounces provolone cheese, cut into thin short strips
- ¼ cup snipped fresh basil

In a small saucepan bring vinegar to boiling; reduce heat. Simmer, uncovered, for 5 minutes or until vinegar is reduced to 3 tablespoons. Set aside to cool.

Drain artichoke hearts, reserving 2 tablespoons liquid; set aside. On 4 long metal skewers alternately thread peppers, cipollini, and mushrooms, leaving ¼ inch between pieces. In a small bowl combine reduced vinegar and reserved artichoke liquid. Brush half of vinegar mixture over vegetables.

Grill skewers on the rack of an uncovered grill directly over medium heat for 8 to 10 minutes or until vegetables are tender, turning once and brushing often with remaining vinegar mixture. Remove vegetables from skewers and transfer to a large bowl; add drained artichokes, cheese, and basil. Season with salt and pepper to taste. Toss gently to combine.

Nutrition facts per serving: 106 cal., 4 g total fat (2 g sat. fat), 7 mg chol., 220 mg sodium, 14 gcarbo., 1 g fiber, 4 g pro. Daily values: 18% vit. A, 94% vit. C, 7% calcium, 9% iron

# spicy potato slices

**Potatoes with a buttery yellow flesh, such as Yukon gold or Finnish yellow, are ideal for this dish. The spices are a nice contrast to their moist, creamy texture. Gild the lily with a little light sour cream and snipped chives, if you like.**



- **1 teaspoon dried thyme, crushed**
- **½ teaspoon paprika**
- **½ teaspoon garlic salt**
- **⅛ teaspoon freshly ground black pepper**
- **3 large yellow potatoes or 2 russet potatoes, scrubbed (about 1 pound)**
- **1 sweet onion (such as Vidalia or Walla Walla), sliced**
- **2 tablespoons olive oil**
- **¼ cup light dairy sour cream (optional)**
- **1 tablespoon snipped fresh chives (optional)**

**Prep: 10 minutes Grill: 20 minutes Makes 4 servings**

For seasoning mixture, combine thyme, paprika, garlic salt, and pepper; set aside. Fold a 36×18-inch piece of heavy foil in half to make a double thickness of foil that measures 18×18 inches. Cut potatoes crosswise into ¼-inch-thick slices. Place the potato slices and onion slices in the center of the foil. Drizzle with oil. Sprinkle with seasoning mixture.

Bring up opposite edges of foil and seal with a double fold. Fold remaining edges to completely enclose the vegetables, leaving space for steam to build.

Grill on the rack of an uncovered grill directly over medium heat for 20 to 25 minutes or until potatoes are tender. If desired, serve with the sour cream and chives.

Nutrition facts per serving: 186 cal., 7 g total fat (1 g sat. fat), 0 mg chol., 266 mg sodium, 29 g carbo., 1 g fiber, 3 g pro. Daily values: 1% vit. A, 29% vit. C, 1% calcium, 11% iron

# jasmine-mint tea rice with peas

**Here's an interesting idea: You might know that cooking rice in stock or broth gives it extra flavor, but how about in tea? Here, nutty, aromatic jasmine rice is cooked in mint tea—and tossed with fresh mint and peas. Serve it with grilled fish or lamb.**



**Start to finish: 32 minutes Makes 4 servings**

- 1 bag mint-flavored tea
- 1¼ cups boiling water
- 1 cup jasmine rice
- 1 tablespoon margarine or butter
- ½ teaspoon salt
- ½ cup fresh shelled or thawed frozen peas
- 2 teaspoons snipped fresh mint

Place tea bag in a small glass bowl. Pour boiling water over tea. Cover; let stand 5 minutes. Remove tea bag and discard. Meanwhile, tear off a 36×18-inch piece of heavy foil. Fold in half to make a double thickness of foil that measures 18×18 inches. Bring up all sides of foil to form a pouch. Place uncooked rice in center of pouch. Place margarine or butter on top of rice; sprinkle with salt. Carefully pour brewed tea over rice. Bring edges of foil together and seal tightly, forming a pouch, leaving space for steam to build. Grill foil pouch on the rack of an uncovered grill directly over medium-high coals about 25 minutes or until liquid is absorbed and rice is tender. Remove from grill. Carefully open packet. Add peas. Seal packet and let stand 10 minutes. Just before serving, sprinkle with fresh mint.

Nutrition facts per serving: 184 cal., 0 g total fat, 0 mg chol., 270 mg sodium, 40 g carbo., 1 g fiber, 4 g pro. Daily values: 1% vit. A, 4% vit. C, 1% calcium, 16% iron

## nicer rice

Aromatic rices are a bit more expensive than plain white rice, but their qualities are well worth the price. Here's a sampling:

**basmati:** The nutlike flavor of this very fragrant rice comes from the fact that it's aged to decrease its moisture content.

**jasmine:** A Thai rice that's similar to basmati but less expensive.

**texmati:** A cross between American long grain rice and basmati.

**wild pecan:** An aromatic rice grown in Louisiana with a rich, nutty flavor and a fragrance that resembles freshly popped popcorn.

# warm asparagus, fennel, & spinach salad

**This beautiful and sophisticated green-on-green salad may be monochromatic to the eye, but its components distinguish themselves on the palate: mild, licoricelike fennel; a variety of mixed greens; and tender, smoky-sweet asparagus.**



**Prep:** 10 minutes **Microwave:** 4 minutes
**Grill:** 12 minutes **Makes** 4 servings

- 1 medium fennel bulb (about 1 pound)
- 2 tablespoons water
- 2 tablespoons olive oil
- ¼ teaspoon finely shredded lemon peel
- 4 teaspoons lemon juice
- 8 ounces asparagus spears, trimmed
- 4 cups fresh spinach
- ¼ cup shredded Parmesan cheese (1 ounce)
- 1 tablespoon thinly sliced fresh basil

Trim off stem end of fennel; quarter fennel but do not remove core. Place fennel in a small microwave-safe dish or pie plate. Add the water. Cover with vented plastic wrap. Microwave on 100% power (high) about 4 minutes or until nearly tender; drain.

Meanwhile, for dressing, in small bowl combine oil, lemon peel, lemon juice, ¼ teaspoon salt, and ⅛ teaspoon pepper; whisk until smooth. Brush fennel and asparagus with 1 tablespoon of the dressing; set remaining dressing aside.

Grill fennel on the rack of an uncovered grill directly over medium heat for 5 minutes, turning occasionally. Add asparagus to the grill; grill vegetables for 7 to 8 minutes more or until vegetables are tender, turning occasionally.

Transfer fennel to a cutting board; cool slightly and slice into ¼- to ½-inch-thick slices, discarding core. Divide fennel and asparagus among 4 dinner plates. Arrange spinach on top. Drizzle with remaining dressing. Top with Parmesan cheese and basil.

Nutrition facts per serving: 111 cal., 9 g total fat (1 g sat. fat), 5 mg chol., 231 mg sodium, 5 g carbo., 7 g fiber, 4 g pro. Daily values: 4% vit. A, 23% vit. C, 7% calcium, 3% iron

# honey-glazed bananas

**Take bananas beyond the lunch box! A little bit sweet and buttery, a little bit tongue-tingling, these grilled bananas are terrific with grilled island-style fish, such as Sea Bass with Black Bean & Avocado Relish (page 134).**



- **2 tablespoons margarine or butter, melted**
- **1 tablespoon honey**
- **1 teaspoon white vinegar**
- **⅛ teaspoon ground red pepper**
- **2 large ripe, yet firm, bananas or plantains**

**Prep: 5 minutes Grill: 4 minutes Makes 4 servings**

In a small bowl combine margarine, honey, vinegar, and red pepper. Peel bananas or plantains; cut in half lengthwise. Brush generously with honey mixture. Grill on the rack of an uncovered grill directly over medium heat about 4 minutes for bananas (8 minutes for plantains) or until browned and warmed through; turn once and brush often with remaining honey mixture.

Nutrition facts per serving: 133 cal., 6 g total fat (1 g sat. fat), 0 mg chol., 68 mg sodium, 21 g carbo., 1 g fiber, 1 g pro. Daily values: 7% vit. A, 10% vit. C, 1% iron

## yes, we cook with bananas!

Bananas or plantains (a large, firm Latin American variety) can be cooked in various stages of ripeness, but are best for the grill when they are ripe yet still firm. For bananas, this means when they are an overall yellow color with a few brown speckles and slightly green tips. Plantains take about a week at room temperature to turn from totally green to yellow-brown and another week or two until they're black and fully ripe. They grill best when they're somewhere between almost black and black.

# sweet & spicy pepper-pineapple salsa

**To make this colorful salsa quickly, buy the peeled fresh pineapple that's available now in most grocery stores. The zippy condiment perks up grilled beef (try it with Jerk London Broil, page 97) and pork particularly well.**



**Prep: 15 minutes Grill: 13 minutes Makes 6 servings**

- 12 ounces peeled and cored fresh pineapple, sliced ½ inch thick
- 2 large red and/or green sweet peppers, seeded and quartered
- 1 ½-inch-thick slice sweet onion (such as Vidalia or Walla Walla)
- ¼ cup apricot jam
- 2 tablespoons rice vinegar
- ¼ teaspoon salt
- ¼ teaspoon ground cinnamon
- ¼ teaspoon ground allspice
- ¼ teaspoon bottled hot pepper sauce

Grill the pineapple, sweet peppers, and onion on the rack of an uncovered grill directly over medium heat for 10 to 12 minutes or until sweet peppers are slightly charred, turning once. Transfer pineapple and vegetables to a cutting board; cool slightly and coarsely chop.

Meanwhile, in a medium saucepan* combine jam, vinegar, salt, cinnamon, allspice, and hot pepper sauce. Place saucepan over heat near edge of grill. Cook and stir for 3 to 5 minutes or until jam is melted. Add the chopped pineapple, sweet peppers, and onion to the pan. Serve warm or at room temperature over grilled meats or poultry.

Nutrition facts per serving: 76 cal., 0 g total fat, 0 mg chol., 93 mg sodium, 20 g carbo., 1 g fiber, 1 g pro. Daily values: 13% vit. A, 81% vit. C, 1% calcium, 3% iron

*Note: *The heat from the grill will blacken the outside of the saucepan, so use an old one or a small cast-iron skillet.*

# piquant grilled broccoli & olives

**Broccoli on the grill? You bet! The grilled flowerets take on a pleasing smokiness and still stay crisp-tender. This intensely flavored side dish goes great with any grilled meat or poultry—or toss it with hot cooked pasta for a vegetarian entrée.**



**Prep:** 15 minutes **Marinate:** 10 minutes
**Grill:** 6 minutes **Makes** 4 servings

- 3½ cups broccoli flowerets
- ½ cup pitted ripe olives
- ½ of a 2-ounce can anchovy fillets, drained and finely chopped (optional)
- 2 tablespoons snipped fresh oregano or Italian flat parsley
- 2 tablespoons red wine vinegar
- 2 tablespoons olive oil
- 5 cloves garlic, minced
- ½ teaspoon crushed red pepper
- Dash salt

In a large saucepan bring a small amount of water to boiling; add broccoli. Simmer, covered, for 2 minutes. Drain well. In a medium bowl combine broccoli and olives. For marinade, in a small bowl whisk together anchovies (if using), oregano, vinegar, oil, garlic, red pepper, and salt. Pour the marinade over the broccoli and olives. Marinate at room temperature for 10 minutes, stirring occasionally. Drain broccoli; discard marinade.

On long metal skewers alternately thread broccoli flowerets and olives. Grill on the rack of an uncovered grill directly over medium heat for 6 to 8 minutes or until broccoli is lightly browned and tender, turning occasionally.

Nutrition facts per serving: 91 cal., 8 g total fat (1 g sat. fat), 0 mg chol., 125 mg sodium, 6 g carbo., 3 g fiber, 3 g pro. Daily values: 13% vit. A, 121% vit. C, 4% calcium, 6% iron

# couscous with grilled vegetables

**Serve this pretty lemon-scented vegetable couscous with something uncomplicated, such as grilled chicken or pork, to show off its lovely hues and fresh flavors.**



- ¼ cup snipped fresh oregano
- ¼ cup snipped fresh parsley
- ¼ cup lemon juice
- 3 tablespoons olive oil
- 1 teaspoon bottled minced garlic
- 1 tablespoon water
- 2 red and/or green sweet peppers, seeded and quartered
- 1 medium red onion, sliced ½ inch thick
- 1 small zucchini, halved lengthwise
- 1 small yellow summer squash, halved lengthwise
- 1 10-ounce package couscous
- ½ cup pistachio nuts or dry roasted peanuts (optional)

**Prep: 20 minutes Grill: 12 minutes Makes 6 to 8 servings**

For dressing, in a small bowl combine oregano, parsley, lemon juice, oil, garlic, and water. Brush the vegetables lightly with some of the dressing. Grill the vegetables on the rack of an uncovered grill directly over medium heat for 12 to 15 minutes or until vegetables are crisp-tender, turning occasionally.

Meanwhile, prepare the couscous according to package directions. Transfer grilled vegetables to cutting board; cool slightly and coarsely chop. Add chopped vegetables to couscous. Stir in remaining dressing. If desired, stir in nuts. Season to taste with salt and freshly ground black pepper; toss.

Nutrition facts per serving: 259 cal., 7 g total fat (1 g sat. fat), 0 mg chol., 32 mg sodium, 42 g carbo., 8 g fiber, 7 g pro. Daily values: 12% vit. A, 67% vit. C, 2% calcium, 6% iron

# grilled eggplant salad

**Few vegetables take to the grill so kindly as eggplant. Its meaty flesh stays firm with grilling, and it tastes delicious with the smoky flavor grilling imparts. You can use the smaller, rounder Italian or baby eggplant in place of the Japanese variety.**



**Prep:** 10 minutes **Grill:** 8 minutes **Makes** 4 to 6 servings

- **3 tablespoons snipped fresh herbs (basil, oregano, and/or parsley)**
- **3 tablespoons balsamic vinegar**
- **2 tablespoons olive oil**
- **2 cloves garlic, minced**
- **3 Japanese eggplants, sliced lengthwise ¼ inch thick (about 12 ounces)***
- **2 medium red sweet peppers, seeded and cut into 1-inch-wide strips**
- **2 medium sweet onions (such as Vidalia or Walla Walla), sliced ½ inch thick**

In a small bowl combine the herbs, vinegar, oil, and garlic, plus salt and freshly ground black pepper to taste. Grill vegetables on the rack of an uncovered grill directly over medium heat for 8 to 12 minutes or until vegetables are crisp-tender, turning once and brushing occasionally with some of the oil mixture. Transfer vegetables to serving dish; toss with remaining oil mixture.

Nutrition facts per serving: 116 cal., 7 g total fat (1 g sat. fat), 0 mg chol., 39 mg sodium, 13 g carbo., 3 g fiber, 1 g pro. Daily values: 27% vit. A, 112% vit. C, 1% calcium, 6% iron

**Note: If desired, substitute 1 small regular eggplant for the Japanese eggplants. Slice the eggplant and grill as above. Before serving, cut the eggplant slices into quarters.*

## eggplant ideas

One of the best ways to prepare eggplant is to grill it, and there's a multitude of ways to use it once the smoky slices come off the grill. Cut it in small chunks and toss it with warm pasta and feta cheese or with rice, garlic, olive oil, and your favorite herbs to make a chilled salad. Roll strips of it in softened lavosh or pita with goat cheese and grilled red sweet peppers and onions, or simply lay a slice on grilled bread and top it with hummus.

# grilled **corn** relish

**Terrific as a side dish for grilled chicken or pork, this colorful corn relish also makes a light meal stirred with some cooked black beans, rolled up with some shredded Monterey Jack cheese in a flour tortilla, then warmed on the grill.**



**Prep: 15 minutes   Grill: 25 minutes   Makes 4 servings**

- **3 tablespoons lime juice**
- **1 tablespoon cooking oil**
- **2 cloves garlic, minced**
- **2 fresh ears of corn, husked and cleaned**
- **1 teaspoon chili powder**
- **1 small avocado, seeded, peeled, and cut up**
- **½ cup chopped red sweet pepper**
- **¼ cup snipped fresh cilantro**
- **¼ teaspoon salt**

In medium bowl combine lime juice, oil, and garlic. Brush corn lightly with juice mixture. Sprinkle corn with chili powder. Grill corn on the rack of an uncovered grill directly over medium heat for 25 to 30 minutes or until tender, turning occasionally.

Meanwhile, add avocado, sweet pepper, cilantro, and salt to remaining lime juice mixture; toss well. Cut corn kernels from cob; stir into avocado mixture.

Nutrition facts per serving: 159 cal., 12 g total fat (2 g sat. fat), 0 mg chol., 152 mg sodium, 15 g carbo., 3 g fiber, 3 g pro. Daily values: 15% vit. A, 51% vit. C, 1% calcium, 6% iron

## all about **avocados**

Silky, buttery-tasting avocados are the base of that famous Mexican condiment, guacamole. Before buying avocados, think about how you'll be using them. Firm-ripe avocados are ideal for slicing and chopping; very ripe fruit is perfect for guacamole and mashing in recipes. Buy very firm avocados if you won't be using them for a few days. They'll ripen at room temperature in 3 to 4 days. Avocados peel most easily when they're firm-ripe. Simply cut them in half (moving the knife around the seed), remove the seed, then peel the halves. For a very ripe avocado being used for mashing, just halve the avocado and scoop the pulp away from the skin.

# sweets on the heat

# nectarine-raspberry crisp

**Chock-full of juicy nectarines and jewel-toned raspberries, this juicy crisp takes full advantage of the best of summer's sweet fruits. If you're pressed for time, assemble it up to 6 hours ahead, then chill until it's time to put it on the grill.**



**Prep: 15 minutes Grill: 20 minutes Makes 6 servings**

- **⅓ cup granulated sugar**
- **5 tablespoons all-purpose flour**
- **1 tablespoon lemon juice**
- **1¼ teaspoons apple pie spice or ground nutmeg**
- **6 medium nectarines (about 2 pounds), pitted and cut into 1-inch chunks**
- **1 cup fresh raspberries**
- **¼ cup packed brown sugar**
- **¼ cup rolled oats**
- **¼ cup cold butter**
- **⅓ cup pecans, coarsely chopped**
- **Vanilla ice cream (optional)**

In a large bowl combine granulated sugar, 2 tablespoons of the flour, the lemon juice, and ¼ teaspoon of the apple pie spice. Gently stir in nectarines and raspberries. Transfer to an 8½×1½-inch round disposable foil baking pan. For the topping, combine the remaining flour, remaining apple pie spice, the brown sugar, and rolled oats. Using a pastry cutter, cut in butter until mixture resembles coarse crumbs. Stir in nuts. Sprinkle topping evenly over fruit mixture.

In a grill with a cover arrange preheated coals in a donut-shape, leaving a 9-inch circle in the center without coals. Test for medium-low heat over the center. Place crisp in pan on center of the grill rack. Cover and grill for 20 to 25 minutes or until fruit mixture is bubbly in center. If desired, serve warm with ice cream.

Nutrition facts per serving: 291 cal., 13 g total fat (5 g sat. fat), 20 mg chol., 80 mg sodium, 45 g carbo., 4 g fiber, 3 g pro. Daily values: 17% vit. A, 23% vit. C, 2% calcium, 8% iron

# grilled fruit kabobs with lime-yogurt sauce

**When you've got a taste for a little something sweet after a hearty meal, these light and refreshing fruit kabobs are a natural choice. Save the leftovers—if there are any—for a breakfast treat with muffins or cereal the next morning.**



- 6 6- to 8-inch bamboo skewers
- 1 8-ounce carton vanilla low-fat yogurt
- 1 teaspoon grated lime peel
- 1 tablespoon lime juice
- ¼ teaspoon ground cinnamon
- 1 small peeled and cored fresh pineapple
- 2 large ripe, yet firm, nectarines or peeled peaches
- 2 medium ripe, yet firm, bananas
- 1 tablespoon melted margarine or butter
- 2 teaspoons lime juice

**Prep: 15 minutes Grill: 8 minutes Makes 6 servings**

Soak the skewers in warm water for several minutes. Meanwhile, for the sauce, in a small bowl combine the yogurt, lime peel, the 1 tablespoon lime juice, and the cinnamon. Cover and refrigerate until serving time.

For the kabobs, slice pineapple 1 inch thick; quarter slices. Cut nectarines or peeled peaches into wedges. Cut bananas into chunks. Alternately thread pieces of fruit on the skewers. In a small bowl combine melted margarine and the 2 teaspoons lime juice. Brush over kabobs. Grill on the rack of an uncovered grill directly over medium heat for 8 to 10 minutes, turning once or twice. Serve kabobs with the sauce.

Nutrition facts per serving: 161 cal., 3 g total fat (1 g sat. fat), 2 mg chol., 43 mg sodium, 33 g carbo., 2 g fiber, 3 g pro. Daily values: 6% vit. A, 39% vit. C, 5% calcium, 3% iron

## desperation **dessert** ideas

If you're short on time, don't desert dessert. Here are some quick ideas:

- Ice cream or sorbet topped with fresh fruit.
- Fresh fruit tossed with honey and sprinkled with toasted nuts (pecans or almonds are good choices).
- Half of a small ripe melon filled with raspberries and topped with vanilla yogurt and toasted almonds.
- A coffee or tea bar that offers a variety of embellishments (for coffee, whipped cream and shaved chocolate; for tea, lemon, sugar, and milk) and purchased biscotti, shortbread, or tea biscuits.

# grilled chocolate-raspberry burritos

**Chocolate on the grill may sound like a mess, but when it's wrapped up in a tortilla with fresh raspberries, it's anything but. Kids will love this dessert—and can help make it, too. (They'll stay sticky-finger free!) Try it with a scoop of vanilla ice cream.**



**Prep:** 12 minutes **Grill:** 8 minutes **Makes** 4 servings

- 4 8- to 9-inch flour tortillas
- 1 cup semisweet chocolate pieces
- 1 cup fresh raspberries
- 2 tablespoons butter, melted
- 2 teaspoons sugar
- ½ teaspoon ground cinnamon

Stack the tortillas and wrap in a piece of foil; grill over medium-low heat about 5 minutes or until warm and pliable, turning packet once. [Or, wrap the tortilla stack in microwave-safe paper towels instead of foil; microwave on 100% power (high) for 20 to 40 seconds or until tortillas are warm and pliable.]

Sprinkle ¼ cup each of the chocolate pieces and the raspberries in the center of each tortilla; fold in sides and roll up. Brush burritos with half of the melted butter. Grill burritos on the rack of an uncovered grill directly over medium-low heat about 3 minutes or until the tortillas begin to show grill marks and the chocolate is melted, turning once. Transfer to a serving platter. Brush tortillas with remaining melted butter. In a small bowl combine the sugar and cinnamon; sprinkle over the burritos. Serve immediately.

Nutrition facts per serving: 361 cal., 20 g total fat (4 g sat. fat), 15 mg chol., 179 mg sodium, 49 g carbo., 2 g fiber, 4 g pro. Daily values: 6% vit. A, 12% vit. C, 4% calcium, 15% iron

# bananas suzette over grilled pound cake

**Here is all the drama of crepes suzette without laboring over the crepes—and no chafing dish required! This elegant dessert is made easily in a skillet right on your grill. For company, garnish each slice with a few delicate strands of orange peel.**



**Prep: 10 minutes Grill: 8 minutes Makes 4 servings**

- 2 medium ripe, yet firm, bananas
- 3 tablespoons sugar
- 2 tablespoons orange-flavored liqueur
- 2 tablespoons orange juice
- 1 tablespoon butter
- ⅛ teaspoon ground nutmeg
- ½ of a 10¾-ounce package frozen pound cake, thawed and cut into 4 slices
- Shredded orange peel (optional)
- Ground nutmeg (optional)

Peel bananas; bias-slice each banana into 8 pieces. Place an 8-inch skillet* on the rack of an uncovered grill directly over medium heat for 2 minutes or until hot. Add the sugar, liqueur, juice, and butter. Heat 1 minute or until butter melts and sugar begins to dissolve. Add the bananas and heat about 4 minutes more or until bananas are just tender, stirring once. Stir in the ⅛ teaspoon nutmeg. Set skillet to the side of the grill rack. Grill pound cake slices on rack of uncovered grill for 1 minute or until golden brown, turning once.

To serve, spoon bananas and sauce over pound cake slices. If desired, garnish with shredded orange peel and additional nutmeg.

Nutrition facts per serving: 292 cal., 12 g total fat (7 g sat. fat), 67 mg chol., 139 mg sodium, 42 g carbo., 1 g fiber, 3 g pro. Daily values: 12% vit. A, 15% vit. C, 2% calcium, 5% iron

**Note: The heat from the grill will blacken the outside of the skillet, so use a cast-iron or old skillet.*

# hazelnut pears

**Sweet, ripe pears are cooked in a cardamom-spiced caramel sauce studded with toasted hazelnuts that's perfect with ice cream or shortcake. Prepare the foil-pack along with dinner, then toss it on the grill while you eat for a sweet and easy finish.**



- ⅓ cup packed brown sugar
- 2 tablespoons butter, softened
- 2 tablespoons light corn syrup
- ¼ teaspoon ground nutmeg
- ¼ teaspoon ground cardamom
- 3 cups cored sliced pears (3 medium)
- ⅓ cup chopped toasted hazelnuts
- Vanilla ice cream (optional)

**Prep: 30 minutes Grill: 12 minutes Makes 4 to 6 servings**

In a small bowl combine brown sugar, softened butter, corn syrup, nutmeg, and cardamom. Set aside. Tear off a 36×18-inch piece of heavy foil. Fold in half to make a double thickness of foil that measures 18×18 inches. Place pear slices in the center of the foil. Spoon brown sugar mixture atop pears. Sprinkle with nuts. Bring up two opposite edges of foil and seal with a double fold. Fold ends to completely enclose the pears, leaving space for steam to build. Place foil packet on grill rack of an uncovered grill directly over medium coals for 12 to 15 minutes or until pears are tender. Serve warm pear mixture with ice cream, if desired. Makes 4 to 6 servings.

Nutrition facts per serving: 289 cal., 14 g total fat (4 g sat. fat), 15 mg chol., 163 mg sodium, 43 g carbo., 5 g fiber, 2 g pro. Daily values: 5% vit. A, 8% vit. C, 4% calcium, 9% iron

# grilled pineapple with sugared wontons

**Get under blue skies and into a slower pace with each bite of this tropical dessert. Juicy, rum-glazed, grilled pineapple is sprinkled with a touch of coconut and a whimsical embellishment: wonton skins crisped on the grill and sprinkled with sugar.**



**Prep: 10 minutes  Grill: 10 minutes  Makes 4 servings**

- **6 ¾-inch-thick slices peeled and cored fresh pineapple, quartered**
- **¼ cup packed brown sugar**
- **2 tablespoons rice vinegar or seasoned rice vinegar**
- **2 tablespoons rum**
- **4 teaspoons lime juice**
- **6 wonton wrappers, halved diagonally**
- **1 tablespoon butter, melted**
- **3 tablespoons shredded coconut**
- **1 tablespoon granulated sugar**

Place pineapple in a single layer in a shallow dish. In a small bowl stir together the brown sugar, vinegar, rum, and lime juice until sugar dissolves. Pour brown sugar mixture over the pineapple; set aside. Place a sheet of waxed paper on a cookie sheet. Lay wonton wrappers on waxed paper. Brush both sides with melted butter. Put coconut in a disposable foil pie pan or on a double thickness of heavy foil.

Drain pineapple, reserving brown sugar mixture. Grill pineapple on the rack of an uncovered grill directly over medium heat for 6 to 8 minutes, turning once and brushing occasionally with some of the reserved brown sugar mixture. Transfer pineapple to serving bowls. Place the wonton wrappers directly on the grill rack; grill for 2 to 4 minutes or until browned, using tongs to turn once. Return the grilled wontons to the cookie sheet; immediately sprinkle with the granulated sugar. Transfer the pie pan or foil with the coconut to the grill. Using a pair of tongs, shake pan or foil back and forth about 2 minutes or until coconut is lightly toasted. Drizzle the remaining brown sugar mixture over pineapple; sprinkle with coconut and serve with sugared wontons.

Nutrition facts per serving: 204 cal., 5 g total fat (3 g sat. fat), 9 mg chol., 103 mg sodium, 38 g carbo., 2 g fiber, 2 g pro. Daily values: 2% vit. A, 32% vit. C, 2% calcium, 8% iron

## poultry

If desired, remove the skin from the poultry. Rinse poultry and pat dry with paper towels. Test for desired coal temperature (see tip, page 85). Place poultry on the grill rack, bone side up, directly over the preheated coals (for direct grilling) or directly over drip pan (for indirect grilling). Grill (uncovered for direct grilling or covered for indirect grilling) for the time given below or until tender and no longer pink. (Note: White meat will cook slightly faster.) Turn poultry over halfway through the grilling time.

| Type of Bird | Weight | Temperature | Doneness | Direct Grilling* Time | Indirect Grilling* Time |
|---|---|---|---|---|---|
| **Chicken, broiler-fryer, half** | 1¼ to 1½ pounds | Medium | Tender; no longer pink | 40 to 50 minutes | 1 to 1¼ hours |
| **Chicken breast half, skinned and boned** | 4 to 5 ounces each | Medium | Tender; no longer pink | 12 to 15 minutes | 15 to 18 minutes |
| **Chicken quarters** | 2½ to 3 pounds total | Medium | Tender; no longer pink | 40 to 50 minutes | 50 to 60 minutes |
| **Meaty chicken pieces** | 2 to 2½ pounds total | Medium | Tender; no longer pink | 35 to 45 minutes | 50 to 60 minutes |
| **Turkey breast tenderloin steak** | 4 to 6 ounces each | Medium | Tender; no longer pink | 12 to 15 minutes | 15 to 18 minutes |

**Note: Most recipes in this book are grilled by direct heat unless otherwise noted. For differences in methods, see tip, page 44.*

## **beef, pork,** or **lamb**

Test for the desired temperature (see tip, page 85). Place the meat on the rack of a grill directly over the preheated coals (for direct grilling) or directly over a drip pan (for indirect grilling). Grill meat (uncovered for direct grilling or covered for indirect grilling) for the time given below or until done, turning the meat over halfway through the grilling time.

| Cut | Thickness | Temperature | Doneness | Direct Grilling* Time | Indirect Grilling* Time |
|---|---|---|---|---|---|
| **Beef** | | | | | |
| Boneless sirloin steak | 1 inch | Medium | Medium rare | 14 to 18 minutes | 22 to 26 minutes |
| | | | Medium | 18 to 22 minutes | 26 to 30 minutes |
| | 1½ inches | Medium | Medium rare | 32 to 36 minutes | 32 to 36 minutes |
| | | | Medium | 36 to 40 minutes | 36 to 40 minutes |
| Flank steak | ¾ to 1 inch | Medium | Medium | 12 to 14 minutes | 18 to 22 minutes |
| Ground meat patties | ¾ inch (4 per pound) | Medium | No pink remains | 14 to 18 minutes | 20 to 24 minutes |
| Steak (blade, chuck, top round) | 1 inch | Medium | Medium rare | 14 to 16 minutes | 45 to 55 minutes |
| | | | Medium | 18 to 20 minutes | 60 to 70 minutes |
| | 1½ inches | Medium | Medium rare | 19 to 26 minutes | 50 to 60 minutes |
| | | | Medium | 27 to 32 minutes | 1 to 1¼ hours |
| Steak (porterhouse, rib, rib eye, sirloin, T-bone, tenderloin, top loin) | 1 inch | Medium | Medium rare | 8 to 12 minutes | 16 to 20 minutes |
| | | | Medium | 12 to 15 minutes | 20 to 24 minutes |
| | 1¼ to 1½ inches | Medium | Medium rare | 14 to 18 minutes | 20 to 22 minutes |
| | | | Medium | 18 to 22 minutes | 22 to 26 minutes |
| **Pork**** | | | | | |
| Chop | ¾ inch | Medium | Medium | 8 to 11 minutes | 20 to 24 minutes |
| | 1¼ to 1½ inches | Medium | Medium | 25 to 30 minutes | 35 to 40 minutes |
| **Lamb** | | | | | |
| Chop | 1 inch | Medium | Medium rare | 10 to 14 minutes | 16 to 18 minutes |
| | | Medium | 14 to 16 minutes | 18 to 20 minutes | |
| **Kabobs** | 1-inch cubes | Medium | Medium | 12 to 14 minutes | |

**Note: Most recipes in this book are grilled by direct heat unless otherwise noted. For differences in methods, see tip page 44.*
***Note: Pork should be cooked until juices run clear.*

## fish & seafood

Thaw fish or shellfish, if frozen. Test for desired temperature (see tip, page 85). For fish fillets, place in a well-greased grill basket. For fish steaks and whole fish, grease the grill rack. Place the fish on the rack directly over the preheated coals (for direct grilling) or over a drip pan (for indirect grilling). Grill (uncovered for direct grilling or covered for indirect grilling), for the time given below or until the fish just begins to flake easily when tested with a fork; scallops and shrimp should look opaque. Turn the fish over halfway through the grilling time. If desired, brush fish with melted margarine or butter.



| Form of Fish | Weight, Size, or Thickness | Temperature | Doneness | Direct Grilling* Time | Indirect Grilling Time |
|---|---|---|---|---|---|
| **Dressed fish** | ½ to 1½ pounds | Medium | Flakes | 7 to 9 minutes per ½ pound | 20 to 25 minutes per ½ pound |
| **Fillets, steaks, cubes** (for kabobs) | ½ to 1 inch thick | Medium | Flakes | 4 to 6 minutes per ½-inch thickness | 4 to 6 minutes per ½-inch thickness |
| **Sea scallops** (for kabobs) | (12 to 15 per pound) | Medium | Opaque | 5 to 8 minutes | 5 to 7 minutes |
| **Shrimp** (for kabobs) | Medium (20 per pound) | Medium | Opaque | 6 to 8 minutes | 6 to 8 minutes |
| | Jumbo (12 to 15 per pound) | Medium | Opaque | 10 to 12 minutes | 8 to 10 minutes |

**Note: Most recipes in this book are grilled by direct heat unless otherwise noted. For differences in methods, see tip page 44.*

## vegetables

Before grilling, rinse, trim, cut up, and precook vegetables as directed below. To precook vegetables, in a saucepan bring a small amount of water to boiling; add desired vegetable and simmer, covered, for the time specified in the chart. Drain well. Generously brush vegetables with olive oil, margarine, or butter before grilling to prevent vegetables from sticking to the grill rack. Test for desired temperature (see tip, page 85).

To grill, place vegetables on a piece of heavy foil or on the grill rack directly over the preheated coals. If putting vegetables directly on grill rack, lay them perpendicular to wires of the rack so they won't fall into the coals. Grill, uncovered, for the time given below or until tender, turning occasionally. Monitor the grilling closely so vegetables don't char.



| Vegetable | Preparation | Precooking Time | Direct-Grilling* Time |
|---|---|---|---|
| Asparagus | Snap off and discard tough bases of stems. Precook, then tie asparagus in bundles with strips of cooked green onion tops. | 3 to 4 minutes | 3 to 5 minutes |
| Corn on the cob | Remove husks from corn. Scrub ears with a stiff brush to remove silks. Rinse corn; pat dry. | Do not precook | 20 to 30 minutes |
| Eggplant | Cut off top and blossom ends. Cut eggplant crosswise into 1-inch-thick slices. | Do not precook | 8 minutes |
| Fennel | Snip off feathery leaves. Cut off stems. | 10 minutes, then cut into 6 to 8 wedges | 8 minutes |
| Fresh baby carrots | Cut off carrot tops. Wash and peel carrots. | 3 to 5 minutes | 3 to 5 minutes |
| Leeks | Cut off green tops; trim bulb roots and remove 1 or 2 layers of white skin. | 10 minutes or until tender; then halve lengthwise | 5 minutes |
| New potatoes | Halve potatoes. | 10 minutes or until almost tender | 10 to 12 minutes |
| Pattypan squash | Rinse; trim ends. | 3 minutes | 20 minutes |
| Sweet peppers | Remove stems. Quarter peppers. Remove seeds and membranes. Cut into 1-inch-wide strips. | Do not precook | 8 to 10 minutes |
| Zucchini or yellow summer squash | Wash; cut off ends. Quarter lengthwise. | Do not precook | 5 to 6 minutes |

*Note: *Because vegetables contain little fat to drip off, they don't require a drip pan. Therefore, timings are given for direct grilling only.*

**By making a few conversions,** cooks in Australia, Canada, and the United Kingdom can use the recipes in this book with confidence. The charts on this page provide a guide for converting measurements from the U.S. customary system, which is used throughout this book, to the imperial and metric systems. There also is a conversion table for oven temperatures to accommodate the differences in oven calibrations.

**Product Differences:** Most of the ingredients called for in the recipes in this book are available in English-speaking countries. However, some are known by different names. Here are some common U.S. American ingredients and their possible counterparts:

- Sugar is granulated or castor sugar.
- Powdered sugar is icing sugar.
- All-purpose flour is plain household flour or white four. When self-rising flour is used in place of all-purpose flour in a recipe that calls for leavening, omit the leavening agent (baking soda or baking powder) and salt.
- Light-colored corn syrup is golden syrup.
- Cornstarch is cornflour.
- Baking soda is bicarbonate of soda.
- Vanilla is vanilla essence.
- Green, red, or yellow sweet peppers are capsicums.
- Golden raisins are sultanas.

**Volume and Weight:** U.S. Americans traditionally use cup measures for liquid and solid ingredients. The chart, below, shows the approximate imperial and metric equivalents. If you are accustomed to weighing solid ingredients, the following approximate equivalents will help.

- 1 cup butter, castor sugar, or rice = 8 ounces = about 230 grams
- 1 cup flour = 4 ounces = about 115 grams
- 1 cup icing sugar = 5 ounces = about 140 grams

Spoon measures are used for smaller amounts of ingredients. Although the size of the tablespoon varies slightly in different countries, for practical purposes and for recipes in this book, a straight substitution is all that's necessary.

Measurements made using cups or spoons always should be level unless stated otherwise.

## Equivalents: U.S. = Australia/U.K.

⅕ teaspoon = 1 ml
¼ teaspoon = 1.25 ml
½ teaspoon = 2.5 ml
1 teaspoon = 5 ml
1 tablespoon = 15 ml
1 fluid ounce = 30 ml
¼ cup = 60 ml
⅓ cup = 80 ml
½ cup = 120 ml
⅔ cup = 160 ml
¾ cup = 180 ml
1 cup = 240 ml
2 cups = 475 ml
1 quart = 1 liter
½ inch = 1.25 cm
1 inch = 2.5 cm

## Baking Pan Sizes

| American | Metric |
|---|---|
| 8×1½-inch round baking pan | 20×4-cm cake tin |
| 9×1½-inch round baking pan | 23×4-cm cake tin |
| 11×7×1½-inch baking pan | 28×18×4-cm baking tin |
| 13×9×2-inch baking pan | 32×23×5-cm baking tin |
| 2-quart rectangular baking dish | 28×18×4-cm baking tin |
| 15×10×1-inch baking pan | 38×25.5×2.5-cm baking tin (Swiss roll tin) |
| 9-inch pie plate | 22×4- or 23×4-cm pie plate |
| 7- or 8-inch springform pan | 18- or 20-cm springform or loose-bottom cake tin |
| 9×5×3-inch loaf pan | 23×13×8-cm or 2-pound narrow loaf tin or pâté tin |
| 1½-quart casserole | 1.5-liter casserole |
| 2-quart casserole | 2-liter casserole |

## Oven Temperature Equivalents

| Fahrenheit Setting | Celsius Setting* | Gas Setting |
|---|---|---|
| 300°F | 150°C | Gas mark 2 (very low) |
| 325°F | 170°C | Gas mark 3 (low) |
| 350°F | 180°C | Gas mark 4 (moderate) |
| 375°F | 190°C | Gas mark 5 (moderately hot) |
| 400°F | 200°C | Gas mark 6 (hot) |
| 425°F | 220°C | Gas mark 7 (hot) |
| 450°F | 230°C | Gas mark 8 (very hot) |
| 475°F | 240°C | Gas mark 9 (very hot) |
| Broil | | Grill |

**Electric and gas ovens may be calibrated using Celsius. However, for an electric oven, increase the Celsius setting 10 to 20 degrees when cooking above 160°C. For convection or forced-air ovens (gas or electric), lower the temperature setting 10°C when cooking at all heat levels.*

# add your own recipes

recipe

recipe

# add your own recipes

recipe

recipe

# add your own recipes

recipe

recipe

# add your own recipes

recipe

recipe

## add your own recipes

recipe

recipe

# add your own recipes

recipe

recipe

Cooking Club of America®